ENCOUNTERS WITH THE PARANORMAL

Volume 2
Goldenrod Showboat Edition

Personals Tales of the Supernatural

Foreword by
Mike Ricksecker

With Illustrations by
Adam D. Tillery

Second Edition:
First printing

Cover Photo: *The Goldenrod Showboat*, February 27, 2016, by
        Mike Ricksecker

A portion of the proceeds from the sale of this book will be directly donated to the memory and preservation of the Goldenrod Showboat artifacts. For more information, please visit:
http://www.goldenrodshowboat.com

HAUNTED ROAD MEDIA

PUBLISHED BY HAUNTED ROAD MEDIA, LLC
www.hauntedroadmedia.com

United States of America

To Captain Bill Menke, Annie, Jake, and especially, Shana.

Acknowledgments

The invaluable help and/or inspiration of the following people is greatly appreciated:

Michelle Hamilton, Cathy E. Gasch, Rob Gutro, Brooke Haramija, Vanessa Hogle, Jason Bland, Jacky Ridley, Penny Scott, Donna Gorton, Judy McCullough, Wendee Whittington, and Cheryal Hussain for sharing their encounters.

Jake Medford for the use of much of the Goldenrod Showboat material in this book.

Shana Wankel for her love and for inspiring me to assemble a second Encounters anthology.

Table of Contents

American History Murdered

(Foreword to the Second Edition)

Mike Ricksecker

"Of all the things that man has made, none is so full of interest and charm, none possesses so distinct a life and character of its own, as a ship." --Henry Van Dyke

"It's so much more than ghosts. To gaze upon a relic is to infuse yourself with everything that relic has come to represent: the people, the era, the ambience." I wrote those words March 28, 2016, just one month after I'd first visited the historic Goldenrod Showboat, and just a few days before we all thought it was going to be scrapped. That's a bit a misnomer -- I actually spoke those words into my phone to be published later -- and, as fate seemed to have it at the time, the Goldenrod was spared from its "demise of a scrap pile death." For the next year and a half, the great jewel of the Mississippi lingered, but all the technology in this modern world couldn't save the great jewel of the Mississippi when an arson fire finally extinguished its storied life during the early morning hours of October 21, 2017.

It was murder. Premeditated and with malice aforethought, the 108-year old relic was torched as if someone was simply lighting up the refuse pile in Billy Joe Jim Bob's backyard. It was the last showboat of its kind anywhere in the world, the last true vestige of early Twentieth Century American life along the

Mississippi River, and now this window into the past is gone forever. No further generations will be able to experience authentic showboat life and soak in true living history as only the Goldenrod Showboat could have provided. It's gone.

We call wonderfully old historic vessels like this "Great Dames," and to those arsonists, I have this to say: Here's what you just did to this Great Dame... Imagine an elderly woman sitting in a wheelchair, worn, but still filled with life and vigor, recanting stories from long ago that only she can tell because no one else is left to tell the tales. Even though her voice may be a little raspy and her eyesight not as crisp as it once had been, she's still the last remnant of a bygone era, an absolute jewel, irreplaceable beyond measure. You doused that elderly woman in gasoline and roasted her alive. May her screams haunt you and the smell of her scorched flesh permeate your nostrils for eternity, you murderers.

If it sounds like I'm taking the loss of the Goldenrod personally, I am. There are others that are taking it far more personal than I -- I'm just one voice of many. During that year and a half that the vessel remained, the Historic Riverboat Preservation Association continued its work and plans were put in place to move the historic showboat back to the St. Louis area, paranormal investigations resumed, and Shana and I were handfasted on the Goldenrod's deck (p. 124) on October 29, 2016. The spirits of the Goldenrod Showboat still had their voices. Then suddenly, in the flick of a lighter, it was gone. The time for lamenting is over. Now, I'm just angry.

This wasn't your crusty grandpappy's run-of-the-mill schooner that had been sitting up on blocks near the decrepit shed in the backyard for the past 30 years. This wasn't something run off an assembly line like everything else in today's cookie-cutter construction society. The Goldenrod Showboat was more than rare -- it was unique. It had character. It had charm. And, most of all, it had soul.

Enough of this senseless destruction. Enough of selfishness and self-interests determining that the last relic of a bygone era can be purposefully destroyed without any repercussions. This isn't even a debate of progress versus history since there is nothing going in the Goldenrod's place except for clear land. No strip malls are going in, no high-rise buildings, no fancy marinas. This was the purposeful obliteration of American history that can never be recaptured. It was murder. May the arsonists roast in hell.

Mike Ricksecker
Ghostorian

Foreword

Mike Ricksecker

Almost everyone has a ghost story.

That was the mantra of the first *Encounters With The Paranormal: Personal Tales Of The Supernatural*, and it still holds true for the book in your hand. Nearly everyone from all parts of the world, from all walks of life, have some sort of supernatural tale to tell. Even many of those that don't believe in ghosts will add an addendum to their initial statement of rejection, "I don't believe in ghosts, but there was that one time..." That one time then becomes this person's launching pad for telling a ghost story.

One of the most satisfying experiences for me as a writer and as a paranormal investigator sharing my adventures with the world through Haunted Road Media (http://www.hauntedroadmedia.com) is when someone contacts me through social media and thanks me for helping them. Many times, I'm initially confused, but then he or she explains that by sharing my experiences I have helped to ensure that this person is not, in fact, crazy.

So many people fear the negative backlash that can ensue from simply revealing a paranormal experience – and understandably so! It wasn't too long ago that we instantly locked away someone that started talking about seeing or hearing things that one would not have seen or heard under "normal" circumstances. Even today, after all that we've been smothered with in the national media and on television about the paranormal world, there are still communities that will shun those that reveal having a paranormal experience. Worse yet, some are still accused of evil witchcraft, sorcery, or trying to conjure demons. Not a month goes by that I don't receive some sort of correspondence that accuses me of trying to communicate with demons, and if I don't stop I'll surely go to hell. Nonsense!

Witchcraft is its own whole discussion for another time, but I'll simply say here that Paganism is not a synonym for Satanism, and it's high time the world becomes educated in that. (No, I'm not a Pagan, but I have a problem when groups of people bash others for something about which they're completely uninformed and misguided.)

If there's one thing to take away from this book for the readers that now possess it, it's that if you have had a paranormal experience or have witnessed something you can't explain, you are not alone. There are many others out there who have experienced the same phenomena as you. Reach out and find those people, and take comfort in the fact that you are *not* crazy!

The other thing I hope you take away from this book, if you don't already have it, is a sense of respect for the world gone by, both in the spirits that had once been human and the places in which they haunt. It's simply the same sort of respect that you'd hope others give you.

In interviews and in my video blogs on the Haunted Road Media YouTube channel, I frequently talk about how we, as paranormal investigators, are walking into locations in which many of these spirits once called home. You would not walk into a living person's house and suddenly demand for them to start turning on lights, slamming doors, or hitting you. These souls are still the same, they just now lack a body. Introduce yourself and offer a handshake. If you know something about the ghosts at the location, talk up something you have in common. It's the difference between being an annoying salesman at the door and a friend who's invited in to chat.

Similarly, the locations themselves should be treated with respect. Far too often, the history and heritage of so many fantastic buildings and structures are obliterated in the name of "progress." I was recently saddened to hear from a friend of a barn built in the 1840s, still in good condition, that was demolished because the new owner wanted to purchase the property and flip it quick after a few renovations. How destroying the barn was "renovating" the property is beyond me. More so, old homes are torn down to make way for new shopping centers or super highways. The site of the first Ricksecker house in Ohio, built by my grandfather's great-great grandfather's own hands, is now occupied by a Denny's right across the street from a mall.

At the back of this book is a small section on the Goldenrod Showboat, built in 1909 and the biggest and most luxurious showboat of its time. Earlier this year it was slated to be scrapped and burned, a smack in the face to its longtime proprietor, Captain Bill Menke, who at 80 years old picked up hammer and nails to rebuild part of the boat after it had caught fire in the early 1960s. The loss of this showboat, a vessel that had been a National Historic Landmark, would have been a loss to an entire era of American Midwest river history. Fortunately, in the ensuing months after a farewell ceremony and the closing of its doors April 1, a deal was finally struck that saved the boat from its peril. Unfortunately, so many other historic structures are not so lucky.

In the spirit of respecting history, a portion of the proceeds of this book will be donated to the restoration and preservation of the Goldenrod Showboat, which will once again find a home near St. Louis, Missouri. Thank you. Your purchase has helped us retain a piece of Americana before it becomes extinct.

Too often the masses forget that most of these spirits once had thoughts, feelings, and desires that did not die with them. Those feelings still remain with them, and one can only wonder what they are truly thinking viewing our world from their spectral perspective.

Certainly, they have their own ghost stories, too. Almost everyone does.

Mike Ricksecker
Ghostorian

Spirit Whisper

Michelle Hamilton

It was the week before Halloween in 2004—what better time of year for a ghostly encounter? I was participating in the annual Halloween festivities at the Whaley House in Old Town San Diego. The Whaley House was built by Thomas Whaley in 1856-1857 to provide a house for his growing family and to operate a dry goods store. The land that Thomas Whaley selected for his two-story brick house had been used to hang Yankee Jim Robinson for the crime of stealing the only rowboat in town. A major crime considering that the town's residents needed the rowboat to bring in goods from passing merchant vessels heading to San Francisco. Yankee Jim Robinson was tall, and his execution was botched and it took the criminal several minutes to expire. One hanging would be enough to create a haunted history, but add to this the death of one of the Whaley's children in infancy and the tragic suicide of daughter Violet Whaley after a failed marriage and you have the perfect recipe for a very haunted house.

For years, guests and staff had reported hearing phantom footsteps pacing the corridors and smelling Thomas Whaley's cigar smoke. The scent of his wife Anna Whaley's lavender perfume could be smelt wafting through the air, and at times tightness around the neck at the thirteenth step on the staircase as if a person was being hung had been reported. All of this activity had led the property to be known as "America's Most Haunted?" For me, the statement was not a question, but a fact. Since starting as a junior docent at the age of 15 in 2000, I had experienced my fair share of ghostly activity. But the events on that night in October 2004 would be my most vivid and dramatic.

Halloween was the busiest season at the Whaley House, and as a way to fundraise for the preservation of the house, SOHO (Save Our Heritage Organisation), the preservation organization that has diligently carried for the house since 2000, organized special tours of the Whaley House. That year was our most ambitious yet. Besides just touring the house in candlelight, the guides and volunteers had staged a performance in the house's theater for the guests. Besides serving as a residence and store, the Whaley House was also San Diego's first commercial theater and the city's third courthouse. Following the performance, the guests were allowed to tour the house at their own leisure to look for the ghosts. A little concerned that the resident spirits might prove a little shy, before the evening's festivities my Mom and I had entered Thomas Whaley's store to have a little chat. We explained to Thomas that he should understand that what we were going to do later that night was for the benefit of the house. That he should understand this, after all he was a businessman and that if he and the other spirits were okay with the program could they please play along with us and have a little fun.

The spirits took our request to heart. For the rest of the night they were present. Cold spots where felt throughout the house, phantom odors were smelt by guests and staff, and manifestations where captured on digital cameras. The staff could not have been more delighted as the guests were thrilled with the program and the paranormal activity. I had never seen so much ghostly activity happening seemingly at once. But the spirits were saving the best for last.

I was standing in the dining room, sharing my stories with two women. It was getting late, almost 11:00 PM the scheduled time for the event to conclude. I was in the far corner of the room with my back to the small wooden doorway that had been used by servants to access the kitchen garden. I was telling the guests about my difficulty receiving calls on my cell phone in the house. I would receive phone calls normally in the house, except for when my Mom was calling to pick me up — it was like the spirits did not want me to leave. Half way through my story, I began to hear a strange popping, rumbling sound. Almost like the rumbling of a motorcycle engine — which was strange as the brick walls of the house were thick and I had never heard outside traffic in that room before, despite being near a busy street.

Brushing off the sound, I resumed my story. As part of the ambience for the night and reflecting on the history of the house, I was dressed in period correct dress with a headdress that had long ribbons. Suddenly, very close to my left ear, so close that I could feel the breath blowing on my ear, I heard a male voice whispering, "SHH SHH HA HA." Or at least that is what I heard it to say. I could even feel the ribbons near my left ear move. I was standing in the corner, so no one — at least no one living — could have whispered in my year. I was so startled I let out a shriek and jumped at least a few inches of the ground. Not an easy feat while wearing a corset and crinoline. The guests that I was talking too saw the ribbons by my ear move and even heard the ghostly whisper. After I had collected my wits, I had a good laugh. After all, it felt like nothing more than a harmless prank and I had asked them to play around with us and have some fun! That brought an end to the night's festivities with the guests and staff leaving the Whaley House that night with memories that would last a lifetime.

Michelle L. Hamilton earned her master's degree in history from San Diego State University in 2013. In her free time, Michelle is a Civil War and 18th-century living historian. Born and raised in California, Michelle now resides in Ruther Glen, Virginia. Michelle is the author of *"I Would Still Be Drowned in Tears": Spiritualism in Abraham Lincoln's White House*, you can follow her at her blog http://michelle-hamilton.blogspot.com.

Pets In Spirit Communicating With The Living

Rob Gutro

Like people who pass, when pets and all animals pass their physical energy combines with their memories, personality and knowledge (what is a soul) and makes a conscious choice to stay here as an Earth-bound ghost, or cross into the light, what I call a spirit. Both use physical energies but they use different emotional energies to manifest and give us signs. Every living thing has a soul and makes the choice for the afterlife.

Pets in spirit communicate with the living in the same ways they did when they were in the physical. They also can do things that human spirits can do, too, like influencing things in nature like birds, butterflies, dragonflies, feathers, etc. to behave oddly to convey a message that they're still around. They can also come into your dreams, make appearances, noises, and come to us in other ways.

I'm a scientist and a medium and I've written two books called *Pets and the Afterlife* and *Pets and the Afterlife 2*, about the many ways pets can communicate. Dogs have the intelligence of a three to five year old human child. Recent scientific studies confirmed that, and confirmed they have the same emotional reaction (and love) that people do, when the caudate of their brain behaved the same way (under MRIs) that people's brains do when they're in the presence of a loved one.

As a medium and paranormal investigator, I've received a lot of messages from dogs and cats on the other side. One grieving dog parent I'll call Sally (not her real name) recently wrote me and said her Saint Bernard had passed and she was grieving. She asked if her dog Rocket was okay and wondered why he hadn't visited her. She wanted to know if Rocket had anything to tell her or why he was taken so soon.

I connected with Rocket, who told me he had already been sending signs, but her grief has blocked them. Grief blocks signs from spirit.

Rocket showed me that he sat around a lot and moved his eyes, watching Sally walk around the house. I told Sally, "He liked to sit still! He kept thinking that you were also so busy walking around over and over! He is around you now although he doesn't seem walk with you. He's doing what he seemed to do in the physical, which is sit in one spot and watch you walk around! Does that make sense to you?"

He said that his body just gave out. He's showing me that his joints were all aching. I'm actually feeling pain in my hips. Did he experience arthritis in his hips? Especially his right hip? That's where the pain seems to be centered.

He is okay. He's healthy in spirit and happy to see you and he can hear you. You'll start picking up on more messages as time passes. Just know he's around.

Sally wrote back and confirmed the messages that Rocket sent me: "*Thank you so much. My baby boy went through so much in his short life. He started hip dysplasia at two years old. Two years later he fell on the steps and damaged his hip. The pain meds caused bleeding, so he was too weak to have a hip replacement. A few months later he had his left hip replaced, and his right hip was broken.*

He went everywhere with me and brought a lot of special people into my life. He did lay in the bed most of the time and just watch. He wouldn't get up unless I was out of his sight too long. Thank you for bringing me some comfort. I needed to know he was whole and no longer in pain. I just wish I could feel him."

Another dog that came through to me described his mom's father (the dog's grandfather) with the favorite clothes he wore. How can dogs do that? They project the image of their person, the dog's grandfather in that case, and I describe it to the pet parent.

The woman was astounded that her dog could show me what her father used to wear almost all the time!

Dogs and cats, like people in spirit can also tell me how they passed and make me feel their pain of passing. When I gave a talk in upstate New York at a fundraiser for Adirondack Save-a-Stray rescue, a woman came to me and was distressed because her dog passed. She wanted to know if her dog was okay on the other side and forgave her. It was then that her little dog came through to me and told me that he ate something out of the trash that hurt his stomach and poisoned him.

The woman was flabbergasted. She said "How in the world did you know that's what happened?" She had come home to find the trash tipped over and rummaged through and her dog had ingested something poisonous that she had discarded. I told her that her dog showed me what he had done and that he said there was nothing to forgive. They were his own actions.

So, if readers are grieving over the loss of a pet, they need to know their pets are always trying to give them signs they're still around. The love they have will always connect them to their pet parents.

Rob considers himself an average guy who just happens to be able to communicate with those who have passed. He calls himself a "medium rare" because he's still learning how to meditate for more messages, but he passes messages on when he gets them. He is also a member of the Inspired Ghost Tracking Team, Hanover, Maryland. He has been able to sketch out what a ghost or spirit looks like and has connected with many people and dogs and cats!

His books include: *Pets and the Afterlife, Pets and the Afterlife 2, Lessons Learned from Talking to the Dead,* and *Ghosts and Spirits: Insights from a Medium* (Retired in Feb. 2015). Available in paperback and E-book on Amazon.com.
Rob's Blog: http://ghostsandspiritsinsights.blogspot.com

Not Welcome

Cathy E. Gasch

Few organizations hold such mystic more than the Freemasons. Their rituals and ceremonies are shrouded in speculation and mystery unless you are a member or a part of their inner circle. Since few people are allowed to see inside their lodges, when a paranormal group I was with was invited to investigate reports of strange occurrences in a local lodge, we were more than eager to go!

The building itself was a stone structure built in the late 19th Century and like many of the day, was furnished in the most ornate fashion of the time. Beautiful dark stained carved wood adorned the doorframes and windows. Wide and ornately decorated staircases led to the upper floors where grand ceremonies were held with a less grand staircase leading to the lower floor and basement.

In many rooms, portraits of former and current grand masters and others of high standing adorned the walls. Bookshelves filled with 100-year old books and documents were lined up in the sitting rooms covered with frayed but stately carpets and both old and new light fixtures hung from ceilings and walls everywhere!

While it was very beautiful inside, the dark wood and low lighting created a solemn feeling and so it wasn't difficult to imagine that the walls held the memories of the hundreds of members and guests who walked the halls, sat in the rooms and took part in the mysterious ceremonies in the large rooms on the upper floors!

I couldn't help but feel a tense atmosphere the moment I walked in. It was almost as though someone was watching us from a distance. The presence didn't feel menacing, just… waiting to see what we were going to do!

We set up a command room on the first floor then split off into teams of three or four to rotate to different floors, each team having a two-way radio to keep in touch with the others. Within a short time, reports of seeing shadows, small lights, hearing footsteps and voices were coming in from almost every member of the group!

As we went from room to room, the feeling that we were being watched never left me. While at that time I still didn't feel anything negative or threatening, "whomever" it was seemed to get closer as the evening went on, and quite often I found myself looking around and behind me.

After a few hours, we took a short break in the command room then a team of us headed to the sub- basement where a few of us had already gotten a few EVPs during our initial walkthrough. The sub-basement was the lowest part of the building and was accessed by a very small staircase from the lower level. It was an unfinished area with original stonework walls and indentations which suggested mysterious doorways!

The lack of light except from our flashlights made the room feel closed in. Despite knowing that there were only us ladies in the area, I could sense that we were still being watched by another presence and this time, even more closely!

We had just settled in to begin an audio session when our team leader realized they had forgotten their two-way radio back in the command room. This radio is important since we were supposed to be in constant contact with the others so they decided to go and retrieve it. Remembering the "buddy system," I followed behind and we made our way back up the small staircase to the lower level.

As we approached the wide staircase that led to the first floor I got that distinct feeling that someone else was behind me and looked around. I could hear the footsteps of the team leader ahead of me but I couldn't hear anything behind me. The room was large enough with some outside light that I could see if anyone else was there… but no, it was just the two of us!

The team leader was rushing and had reached the first floor landing by the time I was more than half way up the stairs. As I was approaching the last three steps, I watched as the team leader disappeared around the corner. Suddenly I got the sensation of someone standing behind me!

I started to look around, expecting to see one of the other investigators behind me, but before I could turn and look, I felt a large hand being placed between my shoulder blades and I was shoved forward with enough force that I lost my balance!

I instinctively put out my hands to keep from falling and my flashlight went flying. My right knee hit the second step and my hands hit the landing rather hard.

I stood up and stepped out onto the landing, rubbing my knee and hands and looked around expecting to see someone… but no one was there! Seeing that no one was behind me, I was shaken.

Realizing that I could have been seriously hurt had I been pushed backward instead of forward, I suddenly became angry and called out, "So…what the hell was that for?"

The sound of my hitting the floor was loud enough that the team leader heard it and came rushing back to the stairs to see what had happened!

After explaining that I had been shoved up the stairs, they made sure I was alright and we then went on to retrieve the radio and telling the others what had happened! As we approached the staircase to return to the basement, the feeling of being watched was still there but this time, the presence was at a greater distance!

I couldn't help but wonder, because I had reacted with anger at being shoved instead of fear, did this presence decide that I wasn't worth bothering with for the remainder of the evening? Good thing… it was a long tiring night and now I wasn't in any mood to be trifled with!

By the end of the evening all the team members had some interesting experiences, me included! We left feeling that this wonderful place had many more secrets to share and I hoped that one day I would return to find out who pushed me!

A few days later, I was listening to my audio clips from that evening and I realized that I had left my recorder on the entire time that the team leader and I had left the others in the sub-basement!

As I listened, I could hear me hitting the stair and calling out but I thought I heard something else inside the whirring sound of a freezer unit nearby and played it back.

I then filtered out the freezer noise and magnified the sound and was startled but not really surprised that just before I was shoved, there was a low male voice saying just one word... "LEAVE!"

Remembering the feeling of being watched all evening then being shoved, I thought that "whomever" it was, had waited for the right moment to let us know they were with us. And that chance came when, for just a brief time, I was isolated from the others! By shoving me, they attempted to discourage me and possibly the others from remaining in the building!

Why? Well, after all, this building was used for ceremonies that, for many generations, had primarily male members. Males who not only discouraged female guests but could also have a total disregard for the female gender.

So, it occurred to me that whoever it was that decided to give me a push towards the front door was letting me know, in no uncertain terms, that despite my treating the building and its institution with respect, that because I was a woman.... I was *not welcome*!

A few years later I was able to return to this building and had some additional experiences but whomever it was that had shoved me up the stairs telling me to leave... this time, knowing I wouldn't be put off so easily. never reappeared!

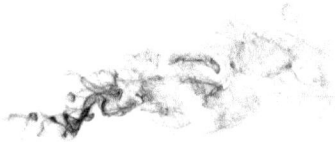

Cathy E. Gasch was born, raised, went to school, worked and still lives in the state of Maryland. She is currently semi-retired and lives in Washington County with her husband of thirty seven years and seven cats. She enjoys working in her yard and garden and enjoys making crafts. Most of Cathy's leisure time is spent reading and researching family history as well as historical locations. She loves to travel and has been to Ireland, Scotland, England and many wonderful and fascinating places in the United States. Cathy's paranormal experiences have spanned over 50 years, and through them, she continues to learn about herself and the world, often times, through the eyes of those who have passed on.

Laptop Lady In White

Brooke Haramija

It was a few years ago, in my old apartment on the South Shore of Staten Island, that one of my most perplexing paranormal experiences occurred. I had been actively investigating locations with the SCARED! team, nearly every weekend at that point. One of the things we were taught is that it was possible to bring spirits home with you. That they "attached" themselves to you, like unwanted Saran wrap, and clung to you for an unknown amount of time until hopefully, without divine assistance, they went their own merry way again. I shuddered to think about it. Thus far, nothing like that had ever happened to me, so I wasn't too worried. But, it was always in the back of my mind. As a paranormal investigator, you do put yourself at risk for certain things. This was one of them.

As I got ready for bed that evening, there was nothing out of the ordinary to warn me of what was to come. My mind was on the latest investigation that we had gone on that past weekend, but nothing was overly scary or foreboding. I fell asleep. Suddenly, I was jerked awake, all at once. Not a nice way to wake up. My body and mind were instantly on alert, the hair on the back of my neck stood up, and my heart was pounding. Nothing had touched me, I don't recall hearing a loud sound, and there didn't appear to be a "trigger" for this instant state of awakeness. My eyes were still closed, even as my heart pounded furiously and I strained to breathe. My muscles tight, I struggled to make sense of the unwelcome intrusion, when suddenly I began to hear noises. I nearly jumped out of my skin until I realized they were coming from my laptop. My laptop, that was closed, in sleep mode, and had been placed upside down on the bed next to me before I had gone to sleep. The noises got louder and more frantic. It was reading the DVD drive and making all sorts of whirring and buzzing noises that should not be happening, almost akin to burning something to a CD (something I had never done before on that laptop). It was like it had come to life, yet without a formal command to do so.

I kept my eyes closed and forced my breathing to remain calm, to try and quell the pounding of my heart. There was nothing to worry about, I reasoned. It was just my laptop, freaking out. And then, just like that, I felt it: a strong female presence, above my head, seemingly coming out of the wall where my headboard rested. How I knew it was female, and coming from above me, I'll never know. And then, with my eyes still closed, I sensed it floated slowly over my body and down to the foot of the bed. I also sensed it was wearing a white dress, and had no legs. Concurrently, an ice-cold breeze blew across my body. That did it. Fully awake and more perplexed than terrified, I reasoned, scientifically, I live in a basement. None of the windows are open. The heat/air conditioning was not on. My door to my room was mostly closed, so nothing should be causing a breeze. Yet, there it was, a truly icy feeling. I was unable to move at that moment, and that is when I started getting scared.

Who are you? What are you? And why are you here? – all questions that came into my mind, but never made it out of my lips. And why couldn't I move? That scared me most of all. The irony of sensing the cliché "lady in white" that everyone talked about at almost every investigation did not escape me. I finally forced myself to open my eyes and sneak a quick peek towards the end of my bed. I had to know if I saw what my brain purported. I sensed, but still did not see, that the spirit had moved there, on the right side of the foot of my bed. She seemed to whisper something I did not catch, (a name, perhaps?) then the feeling was gone as she dissipated. She was gone. I lay there, and the longer I lay there the more scared I got. What just happened? Why did she wake me up? What did she say? Eventually, I had to go to the bathroom, but I lay there as long as I could, thinking it all over, not wanting to get up after this very odd encounter. Finally, I got up and went, a little shaky, to the bathroom in the small apartment. I was never really afraid of the dark, but that night, I practically ran there and back, not wanting to "see" anything and grateful just to get back into bed and pull the covers up once again. Her presence did not seem evil, as I reflected, but it was definitely an unsettled feeling that I had garnered from her, and it reminded me once again of the perils of being in the paranormal field and doing this type of work. Stuff like this could really happen. It also reinforced my belief that spirits can use electronic devices to attempt to communicate with the living. Trying to figure out who she might be, and if she was related to a recent case I had visited or just appeared in my house all on her own, I vowed to protect myself better on future investigations. I found as time went on, the more open I was to seeing and feeling and believing things, the more I would experience. Not surprisingly. So, it was totally possible she was unrelated to any of my previous encounters.

With a little prayer for this spirit's well-being, I was finally able to get back to bed. I never "saw" her again. I still wonder if she had tried to relay a message to me that night. Perhaps one day, I'll know.

Brooke is an actor, singer, writer, stage manager, producer and the proud creator of Brooke's Nook, a vintage toy business that travels up and down the east coast selling unique items and offering free childhood memories to all that come and visit. A self-proclaimed jack-of-all-trades, Brooke also has eight years of experience in the paranormal field, and considers herself very open minded when things go bump in the night.
www.BrookesNookVintage.com

Impressions Of The Mudd House

Mike Ricksecker

The chill of the night air flooded the old farmhouse at the ungodly hour of 4 a.m. on April 15, 1865. The strange man at the door claimed he was looking for medical attention for his friend, Mr. Tyler, who had broken his leg. Hesitant at first given the odd hour of the call, Dr. Samuel Mudd ushered the two men inside and, in the process, ushered in a complete change in the course of his life.

"Mr. Tyler" was not the man's name. This was, in fact, John Wilkes Booth, and the United States authorities were hunting him. The man who had knocked at the door of the Mudd house in Charles County was Booth's accomplice, David Herold, and they were both wearing makeshift disguises. They had just ridden south on horseback from the house of Mary Surratt and her son, John, where they had picked up supplies for their flight out of Washington, D.C. Booth couldn't ride much longer with the leg misplaced from his jump out of Ford's Theater's balcony, where he'd shot Abraham Lincoln, and Mudd's house was on their way out of Maryland. Mudd had previously met Booth, but later claimed that he did not recognize the man that morning.

The doctor set Booth's leg in an upstairs bedroom and tended to his basic needs. After a short amount of rest and recovery, Booth and Herold vacated the farmhouse that afternoon with Mudd pointing the way to Parson Wilmer's, their next destination.

Three days later, Lt. Alexander Lovett, an investigator in the Booth escape, called upon the Mudd house to inquire about the man. Mudd insisted that the man whose leg he fixed was a stranger to him, although there were a handful of accounts in which the two had met. Mudd later claimed that on that fateful night Booth was wearing a cloak over his head, a heavy shawl, and bore a mustache.

On April 21, Lovett returned to search the house. There was nothing to be found except for an old boot, which one of the servants had tossed under the upstairs bed. This was the boot Dr. Mudd had cut off Booth's broken leg; it bore the inscription "J. Wilkes ---."

Mudd was taken into custody at Carroll Prison and soldiers surrounded the house while Booth was still at-large. In her own words, Mrs. Sarah Frances "Frankie" Mudd described the scene at the farmhouse when her husband was first taken away:

"A few days later a company of soldiers were stationed on our farm. They burned the fences, destroyed the wheat and tobacco crops; pulled the boards off the corn-house, so that the corn fell out on the ground, and all the corn that the horses could not eat was trampled under their hoofs in such a way as to render it unfit for use. The meat-house was broken open and the meat taken out. All that they could not eat was left scattered on the hillside where they had pitched their camps. A day or so after their arrival my husband's sister came over to see me. She wanted some garden seeds, and asked me to go down with her to the old gardener, Mr. John Best, to get them for her. When we went out no soldiers were in sight. We carried a basket, and the old man tied up some seeds in packages, put them in the basket, and then asked us to go to see his garden. A few moments after we entered the garden we were surrounded by soldiers. One officer came over and demanded to know what we had in the basket. The little packages of seeds were unwrapped, the contents examined. With a crest-fallen look he remarked, 'I thought you were carrying food to Booth.'"

On April 26, 1865, Booth was caught and killed, and the regiment at the Mudd house vacated the premises. However, Samuel Mudd still remained in custody and was tried in the conspiracy of the Lincoln assassination. His life spared by only a single vote, he was convicted and sentenced to life in prison at Fort Jefferson in the Dry Tortugas, Florida.

In 1867, there was a massive outbreak of yellow fever at the prison, which also claimed the life of the prison doctor. Mudd assumed the role and worked hard to get the situation under control. It almost claimed his life, but he was able to treat the sick and set up an environment that allowed the epidemic to subside. For his heroics, President Andrew Johnson pardoned him in 1869.

Dr. Mudd returned to his home in Maryland and lived out the remainder of his years there until he died of pneumonia in 1883.

Almost a century later, Mrs. Louise Mudd Arehart devoted much of her time and effort to restoring and preserving the old Mudd farmhouse while other family members sought to clear Dr. Mudd's name. At her own house in La Plata, Mrs. Arehart had begun hearing knocking at her front door, but when she answered, no one would be there. The sound of footsteps could be heard going up and down the stairs in her hall, and soon after she began seeing the appearance of a man around the property of her house. This figure was always seen in black trousers and white shirt with a vest, the sleeves of the shirt always rolled up to his elbows. On one particular occasion, Mrs. Arehart nearly ran into the man in her house while she was busy putting away silverware — she passed him through the doorway leading into her dining room. Frightened of the intruder, she fetched her dog and took it throughout the house to try and find the man, but he was nowhere to be found. After pondering for some time, Mrs. Arehart finally realized who the man was...her grandfather, Dr. Samuel Mudd.

At this revelation, Mrs. Arehart became convinced that Dr. Mudd had returned in concern over the state of disrepair his old home had fallen. She persuaded her brother, Joe, who still farmed the land surrounding the home, to let the farmhouse be turned into a museum. With the help of local politicians, she organized the Committee for the Restoration of the Samuel A. Mudd House and it became listed on the National Register of Historic Places in 1974. In 1983, it finally opened to the public… and eerie tales have emanated from the house ever since.

Common disturbances at the home include unanswered knocks at the door, disembodied footsteps around the house, and several sightings of Civil War soldiers. A doll in the upstairs bedroom has reportedly flown out of the chair where it normally sits. The room in which Booth stayed has had reports of coughing emanating from it when no one was there, and periodically an impression can be seen in the bed as if someone was lying there. On one occasion, the door to the attic in the upstairs hallway flew open and a strong gust of wind ripped through the second level. Even Mrs. Mudd has been seen looking out one of the windows of the old home.

In autumn of 2008, a group of Civil War re-enactors were camped around the house when they noticed the artificial candles in the windows of the house were still illuminated. A few of them went inside to put out the candles by loosening the bulbs, but when they returned to their positions, they noticed the lights were still on. They went back and removed the batteries from the candles, but a half-hour later the candles were illuminated once again.

That same season the author's thirteen-year-old daughter had a strange experience at the house. According to her, "The tour guide was showing us some pictures that were hanging up on the living room wall when all of a sudden I felt something pounding under my feet beneath the floor. It was as if someone was knocking at the door, only my feet were standing on the door. Then when we were out back looking at the tombstone, I was just thinking of how nice the breeze was when it felt like the ground lifted from my foot. Someone pushed from underneath the ground and made my foot go up, then they just let go and my foot went flying down."

A return trip was even more revealing... I had somehow lost my original photographs of the house so I made a day trip out there one Monday morning. Much to my dismay, the gates were locked when I pulled up, as I had not realized I'd ventured out on a day the house was closed. However, my timing couldn't have been more perfect. A truck pulled up next to me and one of the staff got out to open the gates. He invited me up since he was already giving a private showing later on.

I explained to him my dilemma with the photographs and he invited me inside while he opened the house. While heading upstairs, I asked him what sort of experiences he'd had on the premises and he explained that he frequently had to fix impressions of a body on one of the beds, had seen Mrs. Mudd staring out of one of the upstairs windows a few times, and on one occasion he heard the voice of Henry Mudd talking to him.

While he tended to the windows in the room where John Wilkes Booth had slept, I looked down at the bed and was nearly floored. "So, this is one of the impressions?"

He spun about and his face flushed when he saw that I was pointing at a human-sized impression sunken into the left side of the bed. "See! That's what I'm talking about!"

I asked to take a few pictures, which he granted, but he remained visibly agitated. "It's not like this when we leave the house at night. Then we have to come up here and fix it to make sure everything looks good for the public."

I was ecstatic with the find. It certainly looked like someone had been lying down on his or her side on the bed, with elbow and feet impressions clearly visible.

Outside near the tombstone, the staff member related some of the previously told stories and admitted that the attention has been a bit overwhelming. A number of paranormal investigative teams have been out to the farmhouse, including The Atlantic Paranormal Society (TAPS) from the *Ghosts Hunters* television show.

Some years later I had returned to the Mudd House for a photo shoot for *Prince George's Suite Magazine*, who was featuring my experiences in their 2013 Fall/Winter issue. While there I decided I would film a few segments for my *Ghosts and Legends* show that I feature on the Haunted Road Media YouTube channel. For years I had been using my digital audio recorder and a clip-on microphone to record the voice for these videos since the camera's microphone does not do a very good job, especially at any sort of distance. I recorded segments both outside on the front lawn and upstairs in the room in which John Wilkes Booth had slept, and was excited at home later to have fresh footage for a new video.

Much to my dismay, the audio recorder had zero files from my time at the Mudd House prior to the photo shoot. I checked the battery of the microphone to make sure it was working properly, and it was, but a faulty microphone recording no sound certainly wasn't the problem. The recorded files that should have been there simply didn't exist although there had been plenty of space on the audio recorder in which to record.

I watched the video segments, perplexed at dilemma and sudden lack of quality footage for my new episode of *Ghosts and Legends*. Had I simply been neglectful and forgot to turn on the recorder? No. Within the video footage you can clearly see me turn on the recorder, yet the files that should have been there simply didn't exist! Once again, the Samuel Mudd House had thwarted my attempts to capture media from the house – first with photos, then with audio.

Of note, the Dr. Samuel A. Mudd Society, a private institution of his decedents that operate the house, maintains that the phrase, "his name is mud," is not a reference to Dr. Mudd and was in use long before the Lincoln assassination.

Portions of this account were originally published in Ghosts Of Maryland, *Copyright 2009 Mike Ricksecker, Published by Schiffer Publishing, Atlglen, Pennsylvania.*

Mike Ricksecker is the author of the historic paranormal books *Ghosts of Maryland* and *Ghosts and Legends of Oklahoma* and the hybrid paranormal research series *Ghostorian Case Files*. He has appeared on Animal Planet's *The Haunted* and Bio Channel's *My Ghost Story*, Fox 5 News (Washington DC) and Coast-to-Coast AM, and he produces his own Internet shows "Ghosts and Legends" and "Paranormal Roads" on Haunted Road Media's YouTube channel. Additionally, Mike is an Amazon best-selling mystery author with two entries to his Chase Michael DeBarlo private detective series, *Deadly Heirs* and *System of the Dead*. Visit his web site at: www.mikericksecker.com

The Cafe Of Kampsville

Shana Wankel

The town of Kampsville, Illinois, is where I was raised and lived for the bulk of my life. It's a small, river town that is rich in history and mystery. I had no idea at all just how much energy my hometown was full of until just in the past few years.

When I was much younger, there was a local grocery store that my family and I went to quite frequently. Back then, it seemed like a normal enough place. As the years passed by, I had moved away from Kampsville, but had somehow found my way back in 2007. Things had changed, of course, and that local grocery store had been changed to a consignment store and restaurant. It was not far from the river and sat next door to the local Archaeology Museum. A friend of my mother's, who is now a dear friend to me, ran the business and hired me on as a waitress, busser, and cook.

Things seemed normal, at first. I started noticing random thumps and bumps in the evenings when I was alone in the building. Sometimes, I would fancy hearing footsteps upstairs. I befriended the ladies who worked next door at the museum and we would talk about the things that were going on in the cafe. One of the ladies actually started a job baking for the cafe and she started noticing things going on that couldn't be explained. When the business closed down in 2008, we made a deal with the business owner that involved us helping her to pack up the business and clean house, in return for free investigating rights, and that's how my paranormal journey started.

We started doing a *ton* of research on the building and the property and discovered that the area was loaded with Native American history. In fact, the property was a former Native American campsite, according to research. When the cafe was first created, however, it wasn't a cafe at all, but a funeral home. Many tragic events have happened on this one small piece of land. I believe that many things contribute to the energy, but being on Native American soil, being located next to the river and being surrounded by limestone bluffs, both of those elements being conductors of energy, I think that's why this one small area has paranormal activity that's off the charts.

We did some more research and discovered that before the building was created, there was a large tree that a small boy had climbed up into, fell out of, and died on the property. I've always felt that his name started with a "B," and this was the start of my adventures with the boy I referred to as "Byron."

"Byron," as I called him, was an active little boy. He always spent time upstairs. It made sense, really, because to him, it wasn't really an "upstairs," but a tree. To this day, the mystery still remains about whether spirits actually see what we see in this realm, *or* if they *only* see what their surroundings were in their time, in their realm, and sometimes there's a "crossover."

At any rate, it was very rare in the beginning for him to come downstairs. We had several investigations where a child's voice was picked up on recordings that sounded like a little boy. At one time, we had a visitor to the cafe who had specific "abilities" that allowed her to see and hear him. We were able to capture an event on a recorder of her looking up into the rafters of the building and "seeing" a little boy. She acknowledges that he's there and then you hear a little child's voice say, "I'm falling." It's incredibly sad to think about him reliving those events over and over, if such is the case, and that he has to stay in that dark, abandoned building. I am positive that he's not alone, however, for there are *many* spirits in that building at all times.

One afternoon, I was inside the cafe with the owner who was gathering her things together to make a trip to the bank. I stayed behind, alone, which is something I never did, just to see what would happen. I said, "Hello," to Byron and to anyone else inside the building who may have been listening. I announced that

I didn't have any of my usual "toys" with me and that if he wanted to, he could let me see him and nobody but me would see him. I was standing in the dining room and heard a couple footsteps and a shuffling noise in the kitchen area. There was a ramp leading to it and it was on the other side of the partition separating the ramp from the kitchen where I heard the noise. I walked up the ramp and announced that I would count to three and when I said the word "three" I wanted to see him. I certainly did *not* expect for him to respect my wishes, but I gave it a shot anyway.

Right after I said "three", I stepped into the opening at the end of the wooden partition and looked down. For a second, I had to wonder if I was imagining what I was seeing, because standing before me was a small boy. He was about five or six years old, if I had to guess, based on his height and comparing it to my own young children. He had short, dark hair, and the biggest, widest, blue eyes that I've ever seen on a child. There was most definitely intelligence alight in those eyes, as they tracked my every movement and watched me as I was watching him. I was struck speechless that moment, and continued taking in my fill of his appearance. He was wearing a short-sleeved, white shirt and khaki or light brown shorts that were long in length. His shoes were well-worn and he was also wearing suspenders. I remember saying his name but he didn't answer me. His mouth didn't move at all. Only those eyes stayed with me.

I totally lost track of time and it was almost like it stood still for the encounter. Maybe it did. The energy in the room during the entire encounter was amazing. The air was constantly charged and filled with static electricity. I finally regained a little bit of awareness of my surroundings enough to notice that there was life outside of that room and that I needed to get back to it. The mother in me wanted to take him with me, but I knew that he was likely attached to his surroundings. I would later find out that *that* wasn't entirely true. I had almost forgotten that the owner was still outside. I figured it would be a great idea to warn her that if she went back inside, she might find more than she bargained for. I remember shaking my head vigorously back and forth as if to clear the fog from it and I apologized to the little boy, who stood there for several minutes with me, and told him that I would come back to visit him, if that was ok. I backed out slowly, watching him continue to watch me, and finally turned around to run outside and shut and lock the door behind me. The urge to go back inside was so tempting, but I needed to save it for another time.

In the years to come, my team and I would have *many* encounters in that one, small building, along that sleepy river town, which apparently, isn't so "sleepy" after all. The town is *very much* alive with paranormal activity and the former residents are definitely *not* resting in peace. "Byron" would eventually start following me home and leading all of us into quite a journey into his world. There is still mystery surrounding the property and the area around it, but it's a work in progress.

Unfortunately, I moved away from the area, and my spirits did not follow, which may or may not be a good thing, considering the nature of some of the energy in that area. The building has since fallen on hard times and the elements have not been kind. However, I definitely feel that the spirits are attached to that building and property indefinitely and will continue to contribute their energy. I have faith that one day, the building will open its doors once more and the journey will continue. Stay tuned!

Shana is a paranormal investigator with 10+ years of experience and enjoys the thrill of researching historical landmarks, venues, and the spirits that inhabit them. She's also an aspiring author and an Empath. She's a firm believer in showing spirits respect, keeping their memory alive, and reaching out to them in a way that makes them comfortable to interact. Shana recently joined forces with Mike Ricksecker and Society Of The Haunted, is an active member of Haunted Road Media, and is the Procurer of Music for Enigma Underground Radio.

The Women In
Black Dresses

Vanessa Hogle

I was preparing for my upcoming trip to investigate in Virginia, trying to get everything together and "all my ducks in a row," so to speak. I took a break and lied down on the couch for a few minutes when three women suddenly appeared in my living room. Two were standing in front of my legs, facing away from me, and an older lady was sitting on the arm of my couch holding a cup of tea.

I just lied there in silence, afraid that if I moved a muscle or spoke they would go away. I lied there for a few minutes feeling the warmth coming off the woman's body that was closest to my head. The other two continued to stare ahead, in silence. They were young, maybe 17 years old. The woman was in her forties. They all three wore black dresses with long sleeves, the dresses hanging to their ankles. They looked very prim. Puritan. I could see the shadows play along the angles of the woman's face as she turned and looked at me.

Very clearly, she patted my head and said, "It's almost time, dear. It's almost time." Then they all three disappeared. Just like that.

I sat up and just sat there, dumbfounded. I had no clue what any of it meant. I called my friend, Gwen Clapper from BPI, and told her about what happened. I was going to be investigating with her and her team in a couple weeks and wanted her opinion on it. She immediately thought of some of the areas she had plans on taking me. The time frame fit, as did the clothing the women wore.

I wouldn't truly understand the importance of that visit until I got to Virginia, until I stepped onto a property I have no intention of ever going on again. The house dated pre-Revolutionary War. The pain and sorrow that pulsed from it was almost unbearable. There were bodies I knew had perished there, and the filth that had seeped into the walls from years of repulsive acts. I know these women wanted me to remember. I know they wanted me to become a voice for those who couldn't speak any more. I know, now, they wanted me to tell what *he* did, to warn others that his actions had set in motion years of unspeakable things, that the stain he left on the property may never fully lift and that those who had suffered since were not alone.

When I saw the video of my "walk-through" of the property all I could see was anguish in my eyes. I saw myself crying. I saw myself saying I wanted to leave. These women knew I had been there before, in another time. I think this was their way of giving me the closure I didn't get back then.

Vanessa Hogle is an author, in her own right, an avid blogger and co-host of the successful paranormal radio show "The Edge of the Rabbit Hole." She has communicated with spirits since her youth and uses that gift to work with teams all over the world. Follow her blog at http://hottamalered.blogspot.com

My Shadow Person Experience

Jason Bland

As I sit down to write about my shadow person experience, the thought comes to me, dear God it's been twenty years ago since these events took place! To me it just doesn't feel that it could be that long ago. Maybe my perception of how many years it has been is skewed by my natural denial of growing old, or maybe it's that I think about these events far too often for it to have been so long ago. I also wonder why it's taken twenty years to write all this down.

It all began in Michigan City, Indiana, when I was a seventeen-year old kid, out way too late and at a party in the woods. It was the night of my junior prom and all the kids that either didn't have dates or were just too cool to go were at parties like this one… well, maybe not exactly like this one. Why the party was being held in these particular woods I will never know, nor do I know whose idea it was to even throw this shindig either.

My best friend, Lance (one of the "I'm too cool to go to the prom" kids), told me to meet him at this party in the woods behind the old Suburban Lanes bowling alley. At the time I also would have said I was one of the kids too cool for prom, but the truth is I was avoiding seeing my ex-girlfriend there with another guy. The last time I had gone to a dance and saw her with another guy I ended up pissing off my date because I was totally depressed, and by the end of night my date ditched me. So, I decided to join this anti-prom party and meet my friend there.

Lance told me to park at the bowling alley and to follow the train tracks that ran behind the building back into the woods. I remember almost not going when I got to the bowling alley and didn't see anybody in the parking lot. I wasn't too inclined to go walk off into the woods all by myself, but for some reason I mustered up the courage and went. I was reassured by the sounds of voices and music as I made my way along the tracks and could see a glimmer of fire in the woods.

The tracks ran over a bridge where the there was a steep incline that led down into the woods. I followed a trail down the hill and could see shadows dancing in the light of the flickering fire shining through the trees just beyond another set of train tracks that ran under the bridge above.

The music I was hearing was a couple guys on acoustic guitars and some long greasy haired fellow playing a conga. There were probably twenty or more people there gathered around the fire, listening to the music and talking amongst each other. I knew everyone at the party, but I was a bit of a loner and had only a few people I considered close friends. I saw none of those close friends at this gathering.

Lance was one of those friends I was looking for, but he had yet to grace the party with his presence.

I socialized but kept away from the drinking and other not so legal stuff that was going on, because… well I'm out in the middle of woods and I've seen too many B horror movies to feel comfortable doing anything that would make me anymore paranoid than I naturally was.

Someone handed me a guitar at one point and I started playing in this acoustic jam session to bide my time while I waited for Lance to show up. It was while I was playing when I first became aware of a presence in the woods.

I wasn't new to the world of the paranormal and had seen odd things since my childhood. Let's just say I became a quick believer when at the age of five I saw a green floating head fly through the room and terrorize my cousin who was just a month younger than me and I, and we both remember that green head to this day. I think I am able to sense spirits and energy because of weird things like that happening throughout my adolescence. That's why I was able to sense something watching us from the woods that night.

As I was playing guitar, I kept seeing out of the corner of my eye movement in the woods. I would turn to look but saw no one there. I was expecting it to be Lance the first time it made me look, but knew after a couple more times that it was something else… a presence. I knew the feeling of being watched, and it was getting stronger as we continued play in the jam session.

Eventually the other guys in this hippie acoustic jam session turned to me to start off with a song. I think one of them noticed I was distracted and thought maybe I would like to lead with something more to my taste. It was the 90s and I was in a grunge band and not into Phish or the Grateful Dead like my fellow musicians. I figured I would play a song from the 60s to hopefully appease their retro hippy ears. I had just recently learned how to play "This Is The End" by the Doors. It was an acoustic version I had been playing around with and I started playing the opening guitar riff of the song. The other musicians were digging it too, but as I started singing the words that feeling of being watched grew even stronger.

The song broke into another melodic jam session, and as its rhythm picked up and one guys was soloing his little hippie heart out on his guitar, a train suddenly came roaring down the tracks. It was at this point, where the music seamed to hit it's orgasmic point of jamming, that the train roared over the bridge. I broke off from playing because I saw out in the woods a tall shadow figure step out from behind a tree! I was just frozen staring at it. Time seemed to slow as no one around me noticed what I was seeing. People were transfixed it seemed by the music and the train and not seeing what I was.

It had to been at least seven feet tall as I watched this shadow figure step out and look right at me. I know what I saw was more than just some shadow. It was like a figure made out of a black hole. Just dark nothingness was what I felt. It seemed all the sadness I felt about screwing things up with my ex-girlfriend and her being at prom with someone else came rushing over me in a wave of emotion. In those few seconds that I saw this thing, it brought out the worst feelings I could ever have and then it just stepped behind another tree and disappeared.

The sounds of the train rumbling faded away into the distance and the other musicians brought the song quietly to its end as if in sync with the locomotives exit from the scene. I was sitting there transfixed on the woods, trying to wrap my mind around what I had just seen as the party continued on. That uneasy feeling from before was now full-blown paranoid terror. I decided it was time to leave before either cops showed up or demonic shadow people started coming out of the woods to take us all.

Funny enough, as I stood up and turned to go I saw my friend, Lance, and his girlfriend, Jessica, making their way toward me. Lance asked if I was leaving, and I told him I had a bad feeling and wanted to go. To my surprise, he agreed he wanted to leave too, even though he had just gotten there with Jessica. As we left the party going back through the woods, he began telling me about something weird that just happened as they had followed the train tracks to the woods. Apparently, they were walking down the tracks and kept hearing footsteps behind them. They would turn around to find no one there until the last time they turned to see a tall shadow figure walk across the tracks. They freaked out a little and quickly made their way to the party, both agreeing that they didn't want to stay after seeing that and they were just coming to find me.

We came out of the woods to the other set of tracks that ran under the bridge and I stopped them.

"Did you guys come down the tracks before or after the train that came?" I asked.

Lance told me they came just after the train. As we made our way up the hill I told them about what I had experienced when the train had come by. They were unsettled to hear I had seen a shadow figure just like they had, and Jessica reiterated that she wanted to get of there.

We reached the end of the trail at the top of the hill and started making our way down the tracks. I looked back at the tracks that went over the bridge and realized the other set of tracks down by the woods ran under the bridge making them a cross tracks.

At the time I read somewhere that cross roads were places that were considered gateways to make deals with demons, or something like that I'd thought. Could cross train tracks be a similar thing, I wondered?

We made it back to the parking lot and we ended up going to Dino's which was our favorite place to get coffee in town. Drinking copious amounts of cheap coffee, we talked about our paranormal experiences we have had. Lance talked about how his house was haunted by the sounds of a baby crying coming from a closet in his sister's room and I talked about stuff I had seen like the green floating head. I spent many nights talking about all things paranormal over a cup of coffee with a number of people at Dino's. It closed a few years ago and now is some kind Italian restaurant.

It wasn't until the next school year when I encountered the shadow person again. A few weird things did happen after that first encounter though. A few days after seeing the shadow person I had a strange dream where all I remember was being on the tracks right at the bridge and the shadow person was at the other end. I awoke the next day with this burning feeling on my face. I ran to the bathroom and looked in the mirror and could see on my right cheek was a clear gel in a shape of a circle and about the size of a dime. I quickly took my finger and touched the gel and it fell off my cheek to reveal a red circle. It looked like somebody took the tip of a burning cigar and touched my face with it. I don't know how it got there or if had anything to do with dream I'd had, but I have always had the feeling that the entity from the train tracks had somehow marked me that night. I was also upset about having this perfect red circle on my face because I had just started hooking back up with my ex-girlfriend again.

By the time this shadow person entered my life again it was Halloween of my senior year of high school. I was a lot happier at the time because I was back with my girlfriend, we'd had a great summer together, had a good grunge band called Pirge that I was the lead singer in, and I was starting to think I might go to Columbia College for film school. But one thing that was bothering me were the strange reoccurring dreams of those train tracks where I was standing at one end of the bridge and the shadow person stood at the other.

As Halloween drew near, Lance started telling me he wanted to go back out to the train tracks to see if we would find the shadow person again. I told him, yeah, we should because I was having weird dreams about that place. Lance admitted then he, too, had dreams about a shadow figure beckoning him to go back there. He wanted to go on Halloween, but I couldn't because I had a show with my band. We agreed to go the night after Halloween, instead.

Lance brought his new girlfriend, Corey. Jessica had broken up with him just a few weeks beforehand when she left for college. They picked me up at my house in Corey's car and we made our way to the tracks behind the old bowling alley.

When we walked out to the tracks nothing felt unusual. It was a cloudy night and the temperature was nice and cool with a calm air. We decided we would follow the tracks down to the bridge that Lance and I had been dreaming about. As we started to walk we could hear the sounds of a train coming and could just see a light down the tracks behind us.

We quickly made our way down the short incline away from the tracks before the train reached us.

I watched the freight train pass, the sounds of it rushing by over powering my senses. I started to get just a tingle of that feeling of being watched like I did before. As the train disappeared over the bridge and the sounds of its wheels became more distant, so did it seem like our surroundings became quieter than they were before. The chirps of the crickets had vanished and the buzz of other insects of the night had completely stopped.

Lance noted the absence of sound first. I thought maybe it was just partial hearing loss due to the train passing by. But it was ominously silent now.

We continued on while Lance kept saying how he felt the whole atmosphere had changed and I felt exactly what he was talking about. Corey kept quiet and I could tell she was getting nervous.

When we got to the bridge I could already see we wouldn't be staying long. Both of them were getting more nervous by the minute. I looked around for our shadowy friend who had been haunting my dreams. What I saw was an empty bridge with a murky pond to the right that looked like it could be home to

Swamp Thing. I then noticed something strange sticking half way out of the pond- it was a dead deer that looked like it might have been hit by a train! I made the mistake of pointing it out and that was it for Corey!

"I'm done! Let's go! This place is creeping me out!" she said.

Lance agreed, but I wasn't done yet. I told them they could go, but I was staying a little longer. I wanted answers to why I kept dreaming of this place and the shadow person. They both said there was no way they were going to leave me out there alone. I argued for them to just give me a few minutes.

I stepped onto the bridge, looked down over the edge where the other set track were about sixty feet down, and then decided to step back off the bridge. Something told me not to cross it. That something wasn't the shadow person, but my own innate survival instinct (also known as fear) telling me to not try and cross that bridge. I knew I could see a train a mile away and would be able to get across or comeback in time, but every bone in my body told me there was danger on that bridge and to get off.

I wasn't done though… I decided to call out this entity that I could feel was there.

"Ok, asshole, why have you brought us out here?" I asked. "Why don't you show yourself? You've been in both our dreams, so tell us what the fuck you want?"

Becoming a paranormal investigator years later, I would become aware of a term called provoking, which at that moment, on that bridge, is exactly what I was doing.

Generally, provoking is not thought to be the best idea by most investigators. I like to compare it to being a blind man picking a fight at a bar with a random person. Seriously. Picture yourself going into a bar, completely blind and picking a fight with someone. You either get lucky and meet a happy drunk that lets your insults go without hurting you, or you get a mean drunk that's not going to treat you so nice for your not so nice words. In fact, maybe this mean drunk is s really disturbed individual who decides to follow this blind person home and is going to pick up stalking as new hobby. The blind person wouldn't know this disturbed individual followed him home and was watching him.

Basically, it's thought by provoking you invite negative entities to mess with you and maybe even follow you home. I wish I would have known that then.

I asked my questions out loud, but the crickets didn't even reply. The heavy silence still permeated around us. I waited for something to happen until Lance said he was done and we were leaving. They started walking back down the tracks, and I followed along, but I lagged a little farther behind them. I was feeling that presence like it was walking behind me and I fought off my fear. I kept thinking in my head… *Come on you son of a bitch! Come on show yourself... I dare you!*

We had only walked about fifty feet when Lance turned around, and I saw a look I had never seen on his face- terror.

"Get your ass up here now!" He yelled.

They waited for me to catch up to them.

"I just saw this huge shadow cross the tracks behind you!" he said grabbing my arm "We're done here; let's go!"

We all began walking again but I started to lag behind a little bit again and was right back to telepathic provoking, or whatever you want to call it. I was challenging it and calling it names. Could even my thoughts count as provoking? I think they can.

We hadn't got much further when Lance and Corey turned back around. I think both of them were about to yell at me to get back up to them, but they were just starring with their mouths open, and then before I could say anything Lance yelled, "No!" and grabbed me by the arm and forced me to run down the tracks with him. Corey had already taken off ahead of us and was heading off to the right to the trail back to the bowling alley and away from the tracks.

I yelled at Lance "What happened?"

But he just kept running, and before I knew it we were all back in Corey's car. They both started talking at once.

"Oh my God! What the hell was that behind you?" Corey yelled.

"I don't know," Lance said

"Why did you guys freak out?" I asked thinking maybe they were messing with me, but they both began telling me what they had seen. Corey started talking about a huge black mass behind me and Lance said it blocked the light down at the end of tracks, and that's when Lance saw it come up behind me and it grew to eight feet tall.

I knew they weren't messing with me then because they both were finishing each other's sentences when telling me what they saw.

Corey suddenly looked shocked again. Lance and I both asked her what's wrong. She told us her stomach was hurting suddenly and wanted to go home. Later, I would find out from Lance that she had started her period a week early which she said had never happened to her before.

On the short drive back to my house I was sitting in the back seat and noticed I still felt that heaviness and a feeling the presence was somehow still with me. I started thinking I didn't want to go home by myself and tried talking them into a late-night coffee stop, but they both agreed that they just wanted to go home.

As they pulled into my parents' drive way I began getting very nervous about being left alone. My parents were home, but by the way all the lights were out, I could tell they were both in bed.

I said my goodbyes and watched them pull out of the driveway and take off. I still felt like I was being watched, and that feeling only got worse when I saw the tail lights of Corey's car disappear.

I tried to find my keys and quickly make it into my house, but I could feel the presence behind me as I tried to produce the right key. After what felt like forever, but was only a minute, I got the right key and was inside my house... my completely dark, quiet house.

I made my way to my bedroom, dropping my keys on the kitchen table that sat about five feet from my door. All during the short trip through the house to my bedroom I felt like this thing was behind me the whole time and didn't feel safe until I closed my bedroom door and flipped on the ceiling light.

My feeling of being safe lasted less than a minute when I heard the sound of my keys being picked up off the table and then put back down. I froze with my ear to the door. My parents were not the type of people to get up in the middle of the night, so I had no idea why I just heard my keys get lifted off the table and put back down. I listened for any other sound, and just when I was about to forget about the whole thing, I heard what sounded like the refrigerator door being opened. It had to be my dad… Maybe he was just going to bed and I missed him coming in? I burst out of my room expecting to see him, but all saw was the last seconds of the refrigerator door closing shut and no dad.

I stood there in my doorway trying to understand what had just happened. I went to my parents' bedroom door and could hear both of their distinct snoring sounds. I suddenly got a cold sweat all over my body and just wanted to go to bed… with the TV on… maybe a nightlight, too.

At some point I got over my fear and turned the TV off (I didn't like sleeping with it on) and I soon fell asleep. That was the first night when the dreams I had of the shadow person took on a new direction.

I was no longer seeing the shadow man at the end of the train bridge – I was seeing it at the foot of my bed!

It was hovering over me, and I was completely paralyzed. It was shaped like a person but void of anything but blackness. I couldn't even scream and it even felt hard to breathe. I started to hear the sound of someone giggling in my head, and then the giggling turned into manic laughter that would make the Joker's laugh seem like a baby's squeal in comparison.

There is no way to really describe the terror I was feeling then. Being paralyzed and not able to act on my basic survival instinct to get as far away from the crazy laughing shadow entity, is the only way to understand the utter helplessness I felt.

Now, I am not a big fan of dream sequences in stories, be it in film or in books. So I'm not going to get into detail about what happens next.

What I remember is hearing that laughter and feeling it hovering over me, but I could no longer see… everything was just blackness. I started to see images, and I realized I was seeing my girlfriend, but she was with another guy. I knew who the other guy was – a co-worker of hers I will just call Wilber.

The entity's laughing only got worse as it showed me a scene of them kissing in the front seat of his car. I was never an over-jealous boyfriend, and it never even occurred to me until I saw this that my girlfriend could possibly cheat on me. Yeah, I know she cheated on her last boyfriend with me, but she didn't feel good about it and she didn't let it go on long before she broke up with him. I just couldn't believe what I was seeing. That's all I will say about what it showed me that night because showing me my girlfriend cheating on me was it just getting warmed up. Let's just say it showed some very personal stuff from my past and relished in my fear and disgust at all it showed me.

At some point I woke up screaming and drenched in cold clammy sweat. It was still the middle of the night and I jumped out of my bed expecting the shadow person to be standing in my way as I flipped on my ceiling light.

The room was shadow person-free as I stood there not knowing what to do next. I didn't want to turn the light off, of that I was sure. I didn't even want to lie back down in my bed. It was already early Sunday morning, and I didn't have work the next day, so I decided to watch TV out in the living room until I was so exhausted I couldn't stay awake anymore. I think I ended up watching two movies before the sun was fully up and it was a new day. So began the first of many sleepless nights as well.

I tried calling my girlfriend that Sunday, but she never returned my phone calls. I ended up finding out she went to work later, so I decided to head up there to see her. She worked at a movie theater, and I thought I would go see a movie and hangout just to talk to her.

When I got to the theater she seemed a little off to me and made me meet her outside in her car. Our conversation in the car consisted of her parents telling me she needed some space. All the images from the night before came rushing back to me in gut wrenching horror. She told me that we weren't breaking up, but that she needed some time. I asked her if there was someone else, and she told me no. I wanted to ask her about Wilber, but when she said there was no one else, I wanted to believe her so bad I didn't ask. I still couldn't believe that she would hurt me that way. I told her I was sorry, I would give her space, and that I just came to see her since we hadn't seen each other since the Friday before at school. She wasn't even able to make it to my band's Halloween show because she worked, so it had been at least a few days since we had talked.

That next day at school I caught her laughing and talking with Wilber in the hall. How sick I felt when I saw them together.

Again, I have never been the possessive or jealous type, so instead of confronting them and making a scene, I walked away before they noticed me.

Later I had a class with one of my girlfriend's friends and I tried inquiring about what was going on. I basically found out that there was something going on. I guess Wilber had been trying to get her to go out with him for a while. He worked at the movie theater with her and the other circle of friends who worked there as well had all noticed him flirting with her. I asked her friend what happened with hooking Wilber up with Jamie, who was another worker at the theater. She told me that Wilber blew her off because he really wanted my girlfriend. I remembered my girlfriend trying to play matchmaker with Wilber and Jamie, but I never heard any more about it after she set them up on a date.

All I kept seeing were the images of the two them together as the shadow person laughed at me. A lot of guys would have went and picked a fight right there with the guy actively trying to steal their girl. Again, I've just never been one for it. I believed if somebody wanted to be with you that you don't have to chase off other suitors, because if it's true love no one can sway them from that person. I believed that she would, in the end, choose me and still would, except what the shadow person had showed me.

So I did what you do in high school and wrote her a note. I didn't think I could say what I had to without falling apart. I don't remember everything I wrote, but it was along the lines of, "I know Wilber is trying to take you from me and please just talk to me," blah, blah. She responded in kind with a note of her own, telling me it had nothing to do with Wilber and she just needed to find herself and maybe time apart and seeing other people was the best thing for now, blah, blah… blah.

So that was it. The girl I had spent a whole year trying to get back after I screwed up and dumped her, now had dumped me… and for a guy named Wilber!

The shadow person came back for me again that night, to relish in my pain, I think. It was the same paralysis and night of being fed images of my worst fears and deepest personal insecurities. And of course, it showed me more scenes of my now ex-girlfriend making out with Wilber. This went on for many nights and I started staying up extremely late trying to avoid falling asleep. I finally broke down a couple weeks later to Lance about it, and that's when I found out he was having a similar problem.

Now, when I said broke down, I mean it. I was a crying blubbering mess and Lance was probably the only guy I could really show how messed up inside I was. I know he was worried I was suicidal. He gave me some tough words to snap me out of it, like don't let a girl get to me like this and man up. But when he started to tell me that he too was having weird dreams of the shadow person and it was doing similar things like showing him his girlfriend with another guy and very personal things as well, I suddenly knew that it wasn't just me going crazy!

Now Lance had suffered from night terrors all his life, and when his experiences with the shadow person started, he wrote it off as just being his usual nightmare-filled restless sleep. Now that he was hearing my nightmares were so similar to his, he knew there was something going on.

Lance checked with Corey to see if she was having any nightmares and she did admit to having some weird dreams, but she couldn't really remember them that well. She was having some other weird stuff happen like getting really light-headed at times. One day, she passed out in the middle of one of her classes.

We couldn't figure out what was happening to us. Lance thought we had invited in some kind of demonic force. Me being the agnostic I am, couldn't settle on if it was a demon and still can't to this day. In the dreams it felt almost alien like to me.

After breaking down to Lance he said he was worried about me, so I spent the night at his parents' place. Neither of us had a shadow person encounter that night, but I did get to hear the ghost baby cry.

Lance woke up at the same time I did.

"Do you hear it?" He asked.

I listened and, yeah, I could hear the muffled sounds of a baby crying. Lance got out of bed and went to his sister's door and opened it. He flipped on the lights, which seemed not to even faze his sister who slept like the dead. We went to her closet and I could hear the baby still crying. It sounded like it was coming from inside the closet. Lance opened the door and explained that there was another small door that had access to the attic crawl space. He told me to put my ear to the door and when I did I could definitely tell the cries were coming from inside. When I opened the little door the crying stopped. Nothing was in the attic but a few boxes and no ghost of a baby I could see. I thought I would at least get a good night's sleep being at my friend's house, but hearing that ghost baby cry ruined any chance of that.

Not long after my night at Lance's, things started to get even weirder. For starters, the shadow being showed me my cat dying. I had spent the night at another friend's house (I started sleeping over at my friends' houses often to not be alone at night) and then when I got home the next morning I found out she had indeed died that night. My parents had found her face down in the kitty litter. I loved Patches, and she usually slept in my room with me, but when this all started I noticed she stopped scratching at my door at night to come jump up on my bed, like it was her rightful sleeping spot.

My parents loved Patches too. My dad was so upset that my Mom asked me if I could bury her in the backyard for him, because he just couldn't bring himself to do it. I remember burying her and thinking things were getting so weird that I was actually worried my cat would come back to life Pet Cemetery-style.

Another night, the shadow person showed me my band members all talking about how much they wanted to kick me out. Not long after, my lead guitar player called to tell me the band was breaking up, but a week later the truth of the matter was evident when they had formed a new band without me.

It was like my whole life I had built for my self was falling apart. It started feeling like the shadow person was trying to destroy my life, my sanity, and my soul.

One really sleepless night I snuck outside to have a cigarette. I had been a social smoker for about a year, but now I was up to a pack a day and not caring if it was killing me. It was the only thing helping with my overwhelming anxiety. It was a cool November night and a late winter start. It was an overcast night with no moon to illuminate my backyard. I was just standing there smoking and feeling a little bit chilly, when I saw movement out of my corner of my eye. I whipped my head around but couldn't really see anything. I actually have extremely good night vision and could see my yard and surrounding trees even in the low light, but I couldn't tell what it was I saw. I knew in my heart what

I saw was a tall black shadow figure move off to my left, I just didn't want to believe it. I started hot-boxing my cigarette. I wanted to get back inside at the moment but didn't want to waste a cigarette either. I couldn't smoke that cigarette fast enough and decided to put it out and throw it in the woods.

As I walked back to the house I suddenly I thought I could hear footsteps in the leaves and grass behind me, so I whipped around only to find no one there. I was starting to get annoyed and angry. I began thinking how much I'd had enough of being messed with, and I wasn't going to take it anymore so I lit another cigarette and stood there thinking… *Ok if you want me here I am, come get me!*

I wasn't going to be scared anymore, and I felt like this thing couldn't screw up my life any more than it already had. I wanted to face it head on and I was done being scared… or at least I thought I was done.

"Come on you asshole and show yourself… I'm not afraid of you," I said in a quiet voice that betrayed the bravado I was trying to portray, but I was also trying not to wake my parents. I again challenged it out loud with some more verbally abusive name calling, and just when I thought this thing was too chicken shit to really show itself I saw something move in the woods.

In less than a second of time I went from defiant and angry to all the hairs on my body standing straight up, and my heart was beating so hard it felt like a drum beating in my chest. I watched in complete frozen terror as I watched this seven-foot tall shadow being step out of the woods. It walked up to me slowly as I stood there probably with dumbest look on my face and a cigarette hanging out of my gaping mouth. It came within five feet of me and then just stopped. This was the first time I had seen it this close, and I wish I could describe it more but all I could see was blackness in the shape of a person. It did appear like it had a tall hat on the more that I could see it… almost like it could be Abraham Lincoln's shadow.

I was trembling all over and tried to speak to it, but I think my body was in adrenaline overload and just couldn't get a breath out to even talk. I was just as paralyzed as I had been in the dreams where this thing tortured me. I started to hear its laugh in my head and I prayed just let this be another dream, but I knew it wasn't.

This was real and no dream. I was still scared as hell, probably more than I have ever been in my life, but I also stated to feel angry again. I had challenged this thing and now here I was about to piss myself when it answered that challenge. I had to fight back… I had to show it I wasn't going to be afraid of it and that I had the power to make it leave. Somehow, I forced my vocal cords to come back to life and was able to croak out in a very quiet voice…

"Go away… you have no power over me… I said go away!" I yelled finally able to raise my voice, not caring if I woke up my parents or neighbors at three in the morning. It reacted to my defiance by laughing so hard in my head that it actually made me wince in pain and then it just turned and walked back in to the woods and was gone. I stood there for I don't know how long before I realized my cigarette had put itself out and there was a long tip of ash hanging from it. I didn't bother throwing the cigarette into the woods, like I usually did to hide any evidence of my nighttime smoking excursions. I didn't want to go anywhere near the woods and I just threw the cigarette into the yard and ran back into the house, not even trying to be stealthy, so as to not wake my parents. Luckily, my parents really did sleep like the dead and never heard a thing that night.

After that the dreams seemed to take on an even more negative theme with the shadow person showing me either ways of how to kill Wilber or hurt others that I had felt betrayed me, like my ex-band members or my ex-girlfriend. Those dreams really disturbed me because I am not a violent person or believe its right to hurt anyone else physically no matter what they may have done to me. I may be agnostic, but I'm a Buddhist by heart.

The entity also would make me dream of killing myself. One night it would show me going into the garage and starting the car and leaving the garage door shut. I remember how vivid it was seeing myself die from carbon monoxide poisoning that when I woke up I thought I saw smoke in my room and could smell the gas fumes. It would show me hanging myself, slitting my wrist, or shooting myself. (Luckily, my parents were anti-gun democrats and I wouldn't have that option easily.) The worst one was where I would go out to those tracks and let a train hit me.

I had known two kids that I went to high school with that had killed themselves. One of them was a soccer teammate of mine who had graduated a year earlier and then, not long afterward, turned around and shot himself in the heart over a girl who broke up with him. My mother had worked at the hospital that he was brought to before dying from his self-inflicted gunshot. I remember her coming home from work crying and telling me what had happened and to tell her if I ever felt suicidal. She made me swear to her that I would never kill myself and not break her heart. She told me how something like that would destroy her.

I held on to that promise I made as I started to think about killing myself on almost a daily basis. At some point my mom found me in my room in a complete emotional breakdown. I didn't tell her about the shadow person I was seeing (after a couple months of going through this I was starting to think it might not be real at all and I was just mentally cracking), but I told her I didn't want to live anymore and that life wasn't worth it anymore. She talked to me about how I felt would pass and that the pain I felt over my ex-girlfriend would eventually go away. She made me go to a psychologist to get help and to talk with someone because she could tell I wasn't telling her everything that was going on.

The psychologist wasn't much help since I wouldn't tell him anything more than my depression over losing the girl I thought was the love of my life. I couldn't tell him about the shadow person because I was afraid he would have me committed. I played down how suicidal I was feeling as well. After two sessions with the psychologist I just quit going. I didn't feel like he was helping me at all, and I didn't think anyone could help me at that point.

At around this time my ex-girlfriend wrote a note telling me that she was sorry for how things had gone, that she wanted to still be friends, and that she missed me. I read that note over and over again, pathetically hoping that she might be considering taking me back. We ended up meeting at lunch at the high school and I was so happy to be just talking to her again because I hadn't at all since a month before when I had seen her walking down the hall with Wilber, hanging his arm around her and overly touching her.

What I should have realized was that she wanted something from me. She worked into the conversation that she was going to fail her midterm English final if she didn't write a short story to make up for her failing to pass half the tests that year. Of course, I offered to write one for her since I was always writing something. I was just happy to be the one she turned to for help because Wilber probably couldn't even read let alone write for how dumb he was. I also saw it as an opportunity to maybe find a way to say to her through fiction how I felt, without having to really say it.

I stayed up two days straight writing her a dark horror story (I mainly wrote horror stories back then) called "Killer On The Road." It was about how a guy who is heartbroken over a girl (go figure) tries to kill himself with a heroin overdose, but is brought back to life by a dark shadow being/demon. The demon takes over his body at times and kind of forces him into a road trip back to his home state where his ex-girlfriend is engaged to another man and the demon keeps showing him someone killing them both. He thinks he is going to save his girlfriend, but doesn't realize that the demon is taking him over at times and killing rude people on his road trip to hell and ultimately taking him to kill his ex and her new beau. The story was formed around two Doors songs as well: "This Is The End" and "Riders on the Storm."

I don't think I even thought about it at the time that I played that Doors song when I first saw the shadow entity, but it was what I used for the opening of the story. There was a line as well from "Riders On The Storm" that I used in it, "His brain is squirming like a toad," which to me was actually how my brain felt with only about two hours of sleep I was getting every night. The story ended with the protagonist discovering that the demon had tricked him and instead of killing his ex-girlfriend and her fiancé, he instead kills himself in a supernatural battle with the demon.

With all that I was trying to say to her through this piece of fiction, and how clever I thought I was writing it, in the end she never even read it. She just turned it in and got to pass her class. A couple years later I ran into her English teacher who asked me if I had written the story, because she and two other teachers spent a week in the library trying to figure out from whom she plagiarized it. They knew there was no way she could have written it.

I'm glad now my ex hadn't read the story because it might have scared her. I mean, for God's sake I wrote a story basically about killing her and Wilber! I look now at that story and hate it because it showed what a dark and pathetic place I was in at the time. I felt like the shadow person was leaning over my shoulder and influencing my writing of it, that it enjoyed my imaginings of violence and ultimately killing myself.

After a week of not getting a thank you from my ex for writing the story or her suddenly realizing how much I was hurting, I decided to write her another note. This one basically told her all the dirt I had found out about Wilber and how he had lied about being rich, that he bragged to people that he had slept with her (which I found out that they hadn't), and that his real name was Wilber. Well Wilber was not happy about that. He had tried to act like everything was cool between us even though he had connived to steal my girl, but he now was pissed off that I wrote my ex and exposed his lies.

The next night after the note he confronted me at my favorite coffee place, Dino's. He ended up sitting in my booth, telling me he wasn't leaving until we stepped outside. I was not the person I was a couple months beforehand who would have laughed at his threats and just left. After having the shadow person on a nightly basis showing me different ways of killing Wilber, I was starting to think I might actually do it. We stepped outside and he turned around to say something with his stupid mouth, but before he could utter a word, I decked him in the face. Now I'm was a 5'10 skinny grunge kid and he was like 6'2 and built like a football player- I was definitely outmatched, but that didn't matter to me at the time. I could feel the shadow person with me at the moment and I think whatever happened that night, I wasn't the one in the driver's seat controlling my actions.

I don't remember much of the fight, with most of what happened being a blur. I do know I ended up slipping on a patch of ice and falling during the fight and he used the opportunity to stomp on my face. The weird thing was I don't remember feeling a thing! I got right up like nothing happened to me even though I was bleeding from my nose and lip. I remember there were some of my ex's friends there, and they used to be my friends, too. They kept telling us to stop and I think Wilber was going to, but I wasn't me anymore. I attacked him like an animal, punching him in the stomach as I spit blood in his face. He kept punching me in the face, but I just insanely growled, and someone told me later that I even laughed. Everyone who witnessed it said that I looked insane. Every punch he threw at my face didn't seem to faze me, and at one point I grabbed him by his throat and I remember feeling such wicked glee inside as I felt my hand tighten on his windpipe. I was ready to crush it in my hand when somebody from behind grabbed me and threw me off of him – it was a cop!

The cop stood in between us and yelled at us to stop and I could see the fear in Wilber's eyes. I don't know if that fear was from him thinking he might get arrested or that I was smiling at him as I spit out another glob of blood. The cop looked at me with a little trepidation at how crazy I looked, and he told Wilber to shut up when he tried saying I attacked him. I guess the cop had seen us inside Dino's and saw Wilber antagonizing me and asking for a fight, and then watched the whole fight for some reason and didn't stop it until I reached for Wilber's juggler. I found out this when I talked to the cop years later when I joined the police department. I had thought I wanted to be a cop for a short time but realized it wasn't for me.

The cop told everyone to go home and took me to his car. I thought I was going to be arrested, but instead the cop cleaned up my face and told me next time I'm in a fight I might want to duck more often for my face's sake.

He sent me home and my mother was horrified when she saw me. I wouldn't talk to her about what happened and just went straight to my room. I hadn't been in my fortress of solitude for long when my ex-girlfriend called, concerned about me and apologizing for what Wilber did. She also said that she wasn't happy with me when she saw all the bruises on Wilber stomach from where I had been punching him- I was like are you kidding me! Have you seen my face! She promised me that he wouldn't bother me again and I hung up on her.

Later that night the shadow person came back I think to revel in my misery and because I think it thought it had won. I'm pretty sure that night I had been partially possessed since I remember little of what happened and had to hear how I acted from the other people that were there. They all said I looked completely crazy and not the person they thought they knew, who was a philosophical pacifist.

I saw the shadow person standing at the foot of my bed, but this was no dream because I just had turned out the lights and gotten in bed. The TV was on because at this point I couldn't fall asleep without it anymore, and I could see the shadow person just off to the right of my entertainment center. I sat straight up in bed, noticing I wasn't paralyzed like I normally was in my dreams.

"Get out of my room!" I yelled.

I started to hear that laughter faintly like it was coming from so old tiny radio speakers. I swore I was hearing it with my ears this time. Then the entity slowly retreated backwards and disappeared in to my wall. I didn't sleep at all the rest of the night and the next day at school I roamed the halls like a zombie.

I wanted to talk to somebody about what I was seeing, but Lance was the only friend who knew about the shadow person and he had graduated high school the year before. I didn't want to discuss it with any my other friends at school for fear they would think I was crazy. I couldn't wait to get out of class to call Lance and find out if he was seeing the shadow person like I was. When I got home I found a message on my answering machine from Lance telling me to call him. I hadn't talked to him in weeks because I had been shutting all my friends out lately. I called him and left a message at his house for him to call me back and didn't hear from him until later that night.

When Lance called me back he sounded anxious and asked me if I was still seeing the shadow person. I started telling him I was seeing him all the time, not just in my dreams but when I was awake, but he cut me off and said I needed to come over to his house right away. I asked why, and all he would tell me was that his father wants to talk to me. I thought that was weird, but before I could ask why, Lance said to just get there now and hung up. I was thinking, *Oh, great what have I done to piss off Lance's dad?*

I headed over to Lance's house, and as I walked up the steps to his front door ringing the doorbell, when I turned to see the shadow person five feet from me! Before I could react, Lance opened the door and the shadow person was gone. I told Lance what I just saw, and he believed me. He told me that he was seeing it all the time now, too.

He told me that his parents were waiting for me in the kitchen, and I needed to talk to them. I thought again about what trouble I might have been in that I wasn't aware about. Lance's mom was busy doing dishes, while his dad sat at the kitchen table with a fatherly disapproving look on his face.

His father asked me what had been going on with me and I didn't know how to answer. I looked to Lance, and he told me he had broken down and told his parents everything that had been happening to him with the shadow person and that I could tell them what I was seeing. I didn't feel comfortable telling them everything, so I just told them I had been seeing this shadow person on a nightly basis. Lance's dad nodded his head and then looked at me.

"I want you to swear to me that you will never go back to those train tracks again, and I'm going to tell you why," he said and then he began telling me about something that happened to him the same night Lance, Corey, and I went to those tracks.

That night of November 1st when we were out at those tracks, Lance's dad was at one of his favorite local bars having a drink. He was sitting at the bar minding his own business and getting ready to leave, when a man he recognized as a kind of city vagrant who always walked around town with an old beat box radio, sat down next to him. For some reason that his dad couldn't explain, he suddenly asked this guy, "Hey, you remember those kids who got killed thirty years ago on the tracks behind Suburban Lanes?".

Lance's dad told us as soon as the question left his mouth he was like, "Why did I just say that?" and the guy turned to him with a very sad look and said to him that, yes, he remembered because one of the kids was his daughter! Lance's dad freaked out at hearing this and quickly paid for his drink and offered to pay for the vagrant's as well, and then left the bar feeling very disturbed by what just happened.

When Lance told his dad about our adventure out to those train tracks and how he was being harassed by this shadow being, his dad asked him what night we were out there, and at hearing that it was the same night that he had this weird experience, he began to take what his son was telling him seriously.

His dad told us that not only were three young kids killed on the train tracks and their body parts were found all over the bridge where the train hit them, but that there were a number of other people who had been killed there, as well, by a train.

Neither of us had known that anyone had been killed there. I wondered how anyone could get caught off guard by a train when you can see and hear it a mile away. Hearing this from his father started making me feel even more sick, because one of the main dreams I had was killing myself by going to those tracks and standing on the bridge and letting a train hit me! His dad again asked us to swear to him to never go back to those tracks again and we both did, but I would break that promise a few years later out of pure curiosity.

Knowing this now still didn't help me figure out how to get rid of the shadow person that was haunting me, but one thing I was for sure of, I wasn't going crazy. This was a real, and we had attracted some kind of evil force into our lives.

A few days later Lance went and sought help at a fair from a Reiki master who cleansed his energy and told him that a necklace he wore that had a runic P on it (Lance had bought it because his last name started with a P and he thought it looked cool) was a symbol for an evil entity and that he should get rid of it. He did and told me that he wasn't seeing the entity at night or in his dreams anymore. He told me I needed to see this Reiki master, too, but the fair was gone and I had no idea how to find a Reiki master. I did get a book on Reiki but I didn't understand it or how it could help me. Things might have been over for Lance, but they were not over for me just yet.

It all ended for me a couple of weeks later one night. I was a mess by then and was really starting to consider ending my life just to make the torment stop. I was also extremely angry all the time. I went to bed that night and turned off all my lights and even my TV. I wanted to fight this entity but had no idea on how to do it. Before I lied down in my bed I called out the shadow person.

"I'm done with you messing with me… if you come tonight I will fight you!" I said more bravely than I felt. It wasn't long before the shadow person arrived to take on my issued challenge.

I was paralyzed again with the shadow person hovering over me. I was dreaming again, and it began showing me images, but it seemed to have upped its game of terror. I was seeing my ex-girlfriend having sex with Wilber, childhood traumas that I just can't discuss were being replayed in my mind, and then a very vivid vision of being hit by a train on the bridge. I woke up screaming and ran to my parents' room. I couldn't take it anymore and I just wanted help. I remember going into my parents' room, but they wouldn't wake up as I yelled at them. Suddenly I heard the entity laughter and felt myself flying backwards and was back in my bed. I realized I had still been dreaming. Was I awake now? I sat up feeling my clothes sticking to my body completely soaked through with sweat. I was awake now but the shadow person wasn't done with me.

I heard its laughter again and could see it rise up in front of me and the next thing I knew it pounced on me, throwing me back down on the bed. I was paralyzed all over again and it was putting its black hand into my mouth suffocating me. I began to panic and couldn't escape its grasp. I began to see the ceiling get closer and I realized the entity was levitating me off my bed. I was so high up that I could have touched my ceiling fan if I had been able to move my arms. Then I felt my gut sink as the shadow person threw me back down on the bed. I heard its silky voice say to me, "You are mine," in between its laughs, and then it started to raise me back off the bed again towards the ceiling.

I didn't think I was dreaming anymore. Everything felt so real, and I know this was the most terrified I have ever been in my life. Now I have always been and still am an agnostic, but at that moment I was desperate for anything to help me out of this. I was still paralyzed and couldn't talk as this thing floated me up into the air. I started thinking in my head, "Please, God, help me!". I thought it over and over again and tried to find some inner will or force inside myself to fight off the paralysis this thing held me in. It seemed to hear my thoughts and its crazed laughter turned into a snarl as it through me back down again.

"God can't help you!" I heard its sinister voice scream at me, but I kept thinking over and over again, "God, please help me!"

It levitated me again up into the air and the more I kept inwardly calling on God to help the more it started to make animal-like noises. This time I felt my legs touch the fan and my nose touched the ceiling and I was screaming in my head for God to help. What happened next was so fast but I'm sure of what I saw. There was a bright flash of white light that came from the one window in my room and I heard the entity scream as if in pain. I was dropped so hard that when my body hit the bed I bounced off on to the floor. I quickly got up to see the shadow person look like it was raising its arms to defend itself from this powerful light shining into my room, and then I saw a man step out of the brightness. He had suspenders on and rimmed eye glasses and he took one look at the entity making it explode in a shriek of pain, and it then was gone. The man, who looked to be in his 70s, smiled at me and then the white light and him just vanished in an instant. I immediately got up and flipped my light on but there was no shadow person anymore and my savior was gone, too.

I was so frightened by what had just happened that I didn't want to be in my house, so I left. I knew Dino's opened at 4:00 AM, so I went there and waited in the parking lot for half an hour for them to start their business day. I must have looked like a complete mess to the waitresses that morning as I held my coffee with trembling hands and waited to go to school. I spent the next few months getting up and going for early coffee before school, because after that incident I didn't sleep more than a few hours at night. I was always waiting for the shadow person to come back, but it never did.

Someone or something saved me that night. I had a feeling who the old man was that saved me. I went to my mom's photo albums and found the picture of my great-grandfather, Harvey, and when I saw his glasses and suspenders I knew that was the man who had saved me. He had died the year before I was born, but my mom had a psychic once tell her he watched over us and I think he kicked the shadow person out of my room that night.

Everything started to get better with my life after that. I started dating a new girl that made my ex-girlfriend very jealous – especially when she found out Wilber was hitting on her in a class they shared.

My new girlfriend's mom was interested in the paranormal a little bit and I told just some of what I experienced on those train tracks. She told me she lost a good friend, who supposedly killed himself by laying his head on those tracks and was decapitated by a train. She said she had spoken to her friend the night before and that he had a new job and girlfriend he was in love with and seemed happy, but for some reason he walked out of house and went to the train tracks that were just behind his home and killed himself. She still couldn't believe he would do that, but police ruled it a suicide. I would find out more later about the others who had died on those tracks, but it still never answered my questions about what the shadow person was or why it was tied to those tracks. That year I also started listening to a paranormal radio show hosted by Art Bell, and people were constantly calling into the show and telling about their own shadow person experiences. I could hear there were many similarities to mine own encounter.

I had always been interested in the paranormal, and in 2008 I became a trained investigator. I haven't run into anything like what I encountered during my nine years of investigating, and I really hope I never do.

A year ago, I also started doing a live videocast on YouTube every Sunday night called Paranormal Soup dealing with all things paranormal. I have had a few guests on and callers into the show who have described to me similar experiences with shadow beings, and I always relate it back to what I went through.

Am I still agnostic? I am to a degree, but I definitely don't question the existence of some kind of higher force out there, because something for sure intervened that night and saved me.

I did see a shadow entity, though, two other times in my life. Once when driving down a road at night with my wife we both saw a shadow figure up ahead of us, and before I could speak we both were blinded for about thirty seconds. It was like someone shut the lights off all around us to the point we both were seeing purple in our vision from our eyes trying to compensate to the sudden darkness. My wife screamed (she was the one driving), and then it was gone and we could both see again. What that was we don't know, but the spot on the road where that happened there had been a horrible car wreck, killing three high school kids the previous year.

The other time was in our first apartment when I was sick with the flu. The apartment was haunted and we had experienced a number of things, but one night while I was feeling miserable, in the room we both felt was the most haunted, I saw the same shadow figure appear. I told it to get out of my house and then I saw in the blackness where its head was, a red face start to take form. It looked almost like an animal face. I told it to leave again, and it just disappeared.

My feeling is whatever saved me that night has protected me from it ever since, but I still have that small fear that it could one day, return.

I know now why it took me so long to write this all down. What happened to me twenty years ago was the worst experience of my life and probably the closest I have ever come to losing my mind. I can't stand thinking about how pathetic I was back then and how stupid as well. Going back to those days reminds me of a lot of things I've put behind me, and I never wanted to look back at them. Some days my agnostic mind wonders if the shadow person was just some psychokinetic manifestation of my teenage angst? Or was it the real pure evil that we all fear might be lurking in the shadows and waiting for us on the other side. I don't know and like I said before I think about it way too often for something that happened so many years ago.

Jason Bland has been a trained Paranormal investigator since 2008 but has had paranormal experiences since his childhood. He is the Vice President and investigations coordinator for Midwest Paranormal; a non-for-profit group who focus on residential hauntings and are based out of La Porte County Indiana. With Midwest Paranormal he has captured EVPs, photographic, and video evidence. Jason is also the host of the YouTube show Paranormal Soup airing live every Sunday night at 10:00 PM – 12:00 PM Central. The show features everyday investigators and their evidence as well as reviewing the newest paranormal viral videos and articles on the shows World Wide Web of Weird segment.
You can contact Jason at jblandmidwestparanormal@hotmail.com
mwpparanormalsoup.com.

Jacky's Experiences

Jacky Ridley

I was born in Portsmouth, England, in 1944, but immigrated to Canada in 1966. I am a librarian by profession, but prior to university I had several different careers, i.e. a lab assistant in a school of Pharmacy, research assistant in a hospital, Coordinator of the Canadian Task Force for Preventive Medicine, sales and property management etc. My lifelong dream has been to go to university, having left school originally at age 15. Subsequently, I took three degrees staring in my mid-40's including a Master's degree. I am a life-long learner and have had an interest in the paranormal ever since I can remember. I think if I was younger I would certainly study to become a parapsychologist – and who knows? – perhaps I still might!

My Experiences:
1. When I was 12 my mother died. There was no dad in the picture, so I was essentially orphaned. After being passed around the family a few times my Uncle Bert took me in on a permanent basis. He and his wife, Gladys, and their daughter, June, lived in a big old house in the middle of Portsmouth, England. The house was big enough that I had my own room, even though I had an extreme fear of the dark and even refused to go to the bathroom in the night for fear of walking down the dark hallways. A year to the day

after my mother died I was lying in bed trying in vain to sleep because there was what I can only describe as a kind of "tension" in the atmosphere that was almost palpable. I tried in vain to sleep but tossed and turned fitfully for hours. I started wondering about my mother, and a random thought came into my mind: what time did she actually die? This thought went around and around my head, and the tension in the room seemed to build and build until it reached a peak about 1 a.m. in the morning. I didn't know what it meant, and I was always fearful anyway, so I just shakily pulled the covers up to my eyes. As soon as I did, a poster that I had pinned on the wall above the bed literally slid, not fell, but slid slowly down the wall and fell over me on the bed. At the same moment the poster slid down the wall it was like someone had clicked off a switch because the tension in the room was instantly gone – poof! Just like that. Suddenly, everything was quiet and peaceful again. I looked at the clock which showed 1:15 a.m. I turned over, snuggled down, and instantly fell asleep because I knew I had my answer…

2. A few months later another relative of mine rented a camping trailer for a week in Cornwall beside the sea. I was allowed to take a friend, and we spent the week having a wonderful time swimming, digging in the sand, collecting sea-shells and turning over rocks to see what was underneath. It wasn't always sunny, however, so one rainy morning I was sitting in the trailer with my friend and we started to talk about what had happened to my mother. I said, "I wonder where she is now?" As soon as I said it the cutlery drawer in the kitchen fell open and all the knives and forks rattled – so again I guess I got my answer.

3. I met my now ex-husband a few years after I immigrated to Canada. All his relatives, including his old mum and dad and his brother, Pete, remained in England. One morning,

we were both at work when the dreaded phone call came: "Come home now – dad is dying". We frantically booked what was then called an "emergency" flight, which meant that the prices were discounted for people who could not book weeks in advance. Somewhere over the Atlantic and at about 2:00 AM or so in the morning, our time, I got the strong feeling that "Dad" had passed and we would sadly be too late. And so it transpired – he had indeed died at that time and we had missed the chance to say goodbye. We stayed for a few days while the funeral arrangements were made and took the opportunity to spend some time with old friends and family. The next day we attended the funeral at the local church – a very solemn and sad occasion, of course, with quite a few tears being shed. After the service concluded my husband and I linked arms and walked slowly back up the aisle, followed by the rest of the funeral party. I had my head down as a mark of respect, but something made me look up only to find that there, right at the back of the church, sat an old man with a huge grin on his face. He nodded at me as we passed and I remember thinking how inappropriate it was that he was laughing and smiling on such a mournful day. Later that evening in the pub, we went over some old photographs that someone had brought to show my husband as a way for him to remember his dad. I had never met him myself, but as soon as I was shown the photograph I realized just who it was that I had seen in the back of the church that morning. It was dear old dad enjoying his own send-off and saying his last goodbyes.

4. My daughter's husband, Basel, was a cabby in Toronto, Canada. He was a high-energy character, a typical A-type personality who never seemed to relax or sit still for a second at a time, so in retrospect it was easy to identify the symptoms of an impending health problem, particularly with his heart. He smoked heavily, ate badly, and took pills

to keep him awake – it was a disaster just waiting to happen. However, it still came as a huge shock to us all when he dropped dead at the young age of 38 of massive heart failure, leaving his wife with four small children to bring up alone. There was no insurance policy, but he did have a share in a taxi business that he owned together with several of his brothers. We were hopeful that the brothers would cash out his share to help support the kids. Sadly, this was not the case, and we heard, to our dismay, that they had decided since Basel was dead the business and any proceeds were entirely theirs. There would be no funds forthcoming. Earlier, my daughter had been forced to move out of her house and had come to live with me in London, about 3 hours away from Toronto in Southern Ontario. We decided soon after we got the news about the money that we would make the drive back to Toronto to confront them and demand restitution, so emotions were running high as we left to get to the highway. I was driving my daughter's big old van, and she sat in the passenger seat. As we turned down a secondary road that led to the highway, I saw a small white car coming towards me – which was not remarkable in and of itself except that the usual slight glare that reflects off a car's windshield was not there. As the car pulled alongside us for some reason both my daughter and I turned to look at the driver. We both gasped in unison because the driver of the white car was Basel. There was no mistake. No trick of the light – it was him! As we passed he just looked at us, and we got the feeling that he was projecting something – that the money and what his brothers had done really did not matter one iota in the grand scheme of things. Everything was as it should be and would unfold as it should. Then the car was gone. Neither of us said a word for the rest of the journey, lost in our own thoughts, but we were both at peace. It really did not matter and what would be would be…

Ghost Girl

Penny Scott

They used to call me "Ghost Girl" in grade school. See, I thought it was normal to see ghosts up until then. I was teased quite a bit, so I stopped talking about it. I have lived with the paranormal all my life and feel it's just a part of me. I have been on two paranormal teams in which I have been able to help ease a lot of people's minds that thought they otherwise might be going crazy.

Here is an experience that was one of my scariest:

I lived in a house in San Diego County, California, for at least four years. At the time, my daughter was three years old. There were many weird things that went on, including lights going off and on, voices heard in other rooms and when you would go to that room they would stop, and shadow figures. My mother and brother had come to say with us for a bit and would tell me that when we were gone, even they would hear the voices. My daughter, Brittany, kept seeing a man that she would call "the bad man."

"Do you see him, mommy," she would say.

But I didn't see him. It was very strange because I always see them. So, I would ask her, "Where is he?"

She would point him out, but still, I could not see him. This always took place in the house, so I asked, "What does he look like? What is he wearing? What does he want?"

She told me he was wearing a black suit and a top hat, and that he was always looking angry at me.

I asked, "Why is he angry with me?"

She didn't know.

I also had a dog, and she would stand in the corner of the doorway and growl at nothing. Obviously, this was another indication of a ghost present.

One day, my sister was over and I heard a little voice calling, "Mommy, mommy!"

I thought it was Britt, but then I realized the voice was coming from outside my bedroom window. I was so scared that I just started running to her. Not thinking about the baby gate that I had placed earlier in the front door, I literally crashed right through it, flying up in the air and landing quite hard. It hurt. I hit the pavement hard, and I was lying there, stunned.

My sister came running to the door, and said, "Penny, what are you doing"?

I looked up at her and she was holding my daughter in her arms.

Other times I would be sleeping and I would hear, "Mommy!" I would open my eyes, and nothing was there. I would get up and go to Britt's room to see if it was her, and she would be sound asleep.

At night, Britt would say, "Look at all those white circles!"

She would see them only in the living room, and I assumed they were car lights, reflections. But they weren't.

One night, we were the only two in the house. I had had enough of all this going on, and the fact that I couldn't see the ghost was even more frustrating.

I had the baby gate up in the hallway, and I put Britt to bed. I turned around and she was standing there. I said, "Brittany, go back to bed."

She was really upset and said, "No! The bad man! The bad man!"

I said, "I don't see anything now stop it!"

She then started to crawl over the baby gate, I picked her up and asked, "Where is he?"

She pointed straight down the hallway, then dug her tiny little fingernails into my arms and buried her head into my chest. I was so mad at this thing terrorizing her, that I just yelled, "Ok, you S.O.B.! Stop scaring my daughter! You will reveal yourself to me now!"

Just then I could feel it rushing at me. It went right through the both of us, and all I could feel was ice, all the emotions of this thing, fear and evil. I was praying to God, and when it was finally over, I could feel tears streaming down my face. I was just standing there holding Britt, crying.

After what seemed a long time, it felt warmer in the house. After that, the activity subsided. I'm not sure to this day what that was all about, but it was one of the scarier experiences.

Like I said, I have had many experiences and continue to do so. My daughter and I joke that we never have to worry about moving into a haunted house. Just give it a couple weeks, they will be around!

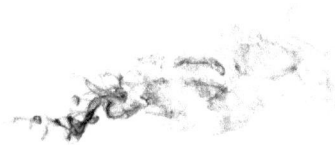

Inside The Salt Circle

Donna Gorton

I've been having experiences since a young child. It wasn't until adulthood I realized I have gifts and am a Sensitive.

I've always had the experience of thinking someone was calling my name. It would drive my mother nuts with me asking at least a couple times a day if she called me, and she never had any of the times I swore I heard her, and it wasn't location-specific. We moved around a lot when I was growing up, and the experience wasn't restricted to where we were.

I also would experience feelings of extreme... anxiety? Fear? Creep-factor? ...over a couple different cellars in two different houses in which I lived. One was when I lived in a house in Nebraska. It was a root cellar, and whenever I was asked to go down for something I just couldn't do it and swore I saw a black mass at the bottom of the stairs when I'd first open the door before turning on the light. This experience happened again in the house I lived in in New York as a teenager... same exact fear, anxiety and panic over having to go down, and same type of black mass at the bottom of the stairs.

Also at the house in Nebraska (we lived there when I was 8 yrs. old), there was a glass door that lead into the living room (you came in the porch door, then the front door and the stairs were directly ahead of the front door; the glass door was directly to the right of the front door). We kept this door shut in the summer to help keep the house cooler. One day I was sitting in my chair reading and my mom, who was working nights at the time, was asleep on the couch. All of the sudden the glass door swung open! It wasn't a slam but like someone had just walked in, so I just thought I didn't shut it tight enough when I came in the room and got up to re-shut it. I sat back down and resumed reading. Maybe a minute later, it swung open again! So I got up again and this time pulled on the closed door to assure myself I latched it shut beyond a doubt. This had never happened before while I lived there.

So I sat back down again and tried going back to reading, but was too distracted and kept a side-eye on the door. And it swung open again a third time! This time I woke my mom up in a panic over it and she just blew it off as a draft. There were no drafts with all the doors and windows shut in the house against the heat! After the last time I got up and left the house to go to my best friend's house next door.

My next experience happened after I moved to New York when I was nine years old. My parents split up and we came to New York to be near my grandparents, but all my mom could afford as a newly transplanted single mother of three was an old single-wide trailer. I had the first bedroom of the hallway. I am the only girl so always had my own room and my two brothers shared.

A few months after moving in, my mom, her new boyfriend and my brothers were going to run to the store for something. It was my bedtime (I'm the youngest), so I stayed home as they'd be back within an hour. So, I went ahead and went to bed.

As I was lying there having just gotten settled in, I heard the sound of the front door opening. My first thought was they had forgotten something and came back. But then as I was getting ready to call out, I heard heavy-boot-sounding footsteps walking around the living room and then the kitchen. Like I said… small trailer and my room was right after the kitchen. The steps grew louder like they were starting toward the hallway! I was *so* terrified someone had broken in! I was too scared to do more than try to cover the sound of my breathing, and I started to cry and burrowed further under the covers not knowing what else to do.

Maybe a few terrifying minutes later, my family came home, and I waited until I heard my mom's voice before winging myself at her hysterical by this time telling her someone had been in the trailer. Her boyfriend grabbed a flashlight and looked around outside for any strange footprints and my mom looked inside for any wet footprints as it was snowy outside. So, if someone *had* come in, they would've tracked snow all over. There was nothing to be found. I can say it was a *long* time before I got to sleep that night!

As I got older, I started getting these random horribly anxious feelings about someone close to me to which something terrible was going to happen. I couldn't shake the feeling! And finally, when I said something to them, they would always reply that everything was fine. I once spoke to a Medicine Woman about this who suggested that maybe it was something happening in an alternate realm than ours. Of course, there's no way to check that, but I also don't have a better explanation for it, and I still randomly have it happen today at the age of 45!

When I was about 16-year old, my mom had hurt her back *really* bad and was bedridden from it. The apartment we lived in at the time had a short hallway with all three bedrooms off it. Hers was next to the bathroom and mine was directly across from bathroom on the opposite end (maybe 8 - 10 feet). I had just come out of the bathroom and passed her room when I suddenly got hit with a vision of her falling down the stairs. I had never had premonitions before, so shook my head thinking she'd not be stupid and try the stairs and continued to my room.

I no sooner stepped into my room when I heard her falling down the stairs! I know there was nothing I could have done as there had been maybe 20 - 30 seconds between seeing this in my head and it happening, but boy I felt guilty for a long time after. The premonitions I've had since have been like that... directly before something happens. Weird!

My Mom was also a Medicine Woman, and as a young adult in my early 20s she began working with me in hopes I would become her successor. She was ever-frustrated that I couldn't do the same things as she. I would say she was more of a Psychic-Medium. Finally, after a couple years I had to tell her that maybe my gifts were just different than hers. But she still didn't do much to acknowledge what I could do.

The house we lived in at the time was pretty old. I was forever hearing the sounds of footsteps upstairs or creaking of floorboards. Upon checking, there was never anything there.

In the room at the head of the stairs was this odd shaped closet. It was wide, but you had to duck down to go inside it and you couldn't quite stand up all the way inside. There was this little door on the side of the closet that I always assumed was just pipe access for the bathroom which was the next room after it. One day, I got curious, though, and opened it when noticed light coming from the side of it. So, I shimmied my way inside and found a little room you could stand up in, and the chimney ran through it. Inside, I found a bunch of illegible newspapers and even one of those old metal wash basins! There was just this *really* creepy feeling in there and I sensed some sort of presence. I got scared and left the room. From the outside of the room there was no way, architecturally, that this room should've been able to be there! I told my mom, and she didn't want to talk about it, quickly changing the subject (which I never figured out why).

In that same house my room was upstairs as well and had a door that led out into a short hallway (the house had been divided into three apartments – we had half the house and upstairs was a small one room apartment, and downstairs on the other side, another one room apartment). This hall just had a bannister that led around to the stairs, maybe ten feet, and I was forever creeped out bad in there. It didn't matter day or night, or if the light was on. So I contacted the town historian who was a cranky older woman who would only say the house was amongst the oldest in town and had been the original creamery for the town. Ok, no help there. So I decided to investigate.

I made a salt circle with a candle inside in the hall and asked whatever was there making me so uncomfortable to talk to me. For the first time ever, it was like a movie started playing in my head! I saw a young woman who lived with her father in the house. He was a drunk and could get violent when drunk. I saw an argument between them where she was in love with a guy of which her father didn't approve. I could see in-depth detail of clothes, colors, and more! She was dressed in early 19th Century dress with a maroon, small flowered high-collared blouse and a long taupe colored skirt. Her hair was in a loose bun. Her father had on a checkered shirt, the sleeves rolled up, wearing tan trousers with suspenders. He had salt and pepper gray hair and longer side burns.

She looked to be maybe late teens... 20 at most. He forbade her to see this guy, which she continued to do anyway.

The young woman ended up becoming pregnant, but her father refused to give her permission to marry her boyfriend. From then on, he refused to let her leave the house and would beat on her if she "acted up." If company came over he used to make her go into the room I'd found so no one would find out she was pregnant. The visitors just thought she either ran off, went away to school, or something of the like. No one asked too many questions back then.

Then it flashed to where she had the baby... a son. One day when she was insisting on leaving with the baby her father went into a rage and started trying to beat her with the baby still in her arms. The fight ended up in the hallway (that freaked me out so badly) and he hit her, knocking her down the stairs backward with the baby, killing them both. I felt all the emotions she had felt. He ended up taking their bodies down by the creek at the end of the field behind the house and buried them there in an unmarked grave. I was just bawling by the time the vision ended. After that experience, I no longer felt any of that stuff in that hallway. It was as if she just needed her story to be told!

Since then there's been many more experiences throughout my life. It was only through research online that I discovered I wasn't alone in what I can do or sense, and that there are names for it. So at least I learned I'm not crazy!

Haunted Halls
Of Ellison

Mike Ricksecker

This article was originally published April 21, 2011, as "A Haunting Investigation Of University Of Oklahoma's Ellison Hall." The members of Society of the Haunted have since changed, although Vanessa and I still remain, she as a remote viewer and Shana Wankel and I serving as the core. I've included it here since we were the first team to have ever investigated this historic building on the campus of the University of Oklahoma.

While ghost stories circulate around the University of Oklahoma's campus, it is rather uncommon for a paranormal team to be offered an opportunity to investigate there, and by all accounts no one had ever investigated Ellison Hall. So when the Society of the Haunted was offered the chance to investigate there, the group's theologian and occult specialist, Chris Borthick, remarked, "This is a very rare and unique opportunity."

For decades, the rumored spirit of a boy who had been mortally wounded roller skating down Elm Avenue during the Great Depression and now skated the halls of Ellison had made the ghost story rounds about the campus. Other sounds, such as people moving down the hallways, have been heard as well but are not as legendary, and staff have witnessed motion activated lights being turned on in hallways and bathrooms when no one else is around. Would Society of the Haunted be able to prove or disprove any of these claims?

Originally named Hygeia Hall after the Greek goddess of health and well-being, Ellison Hall opened in 1928 as OU's infirmary. In the early 1930s it was renamed to honor Dr. Gayfree Ellison, the Director of Student Health from 1920 until his death in

1932. It was during this time that the fatal roller skating accident occurred, and the boy was brought into the infirmary in an attempt to be revived. He died on the operating table. In 1971 the building transitioned to the home of the University of Oklahoma Student Association, and now it serves in a variety of capacities including the Student Services Center, Native American Studies, African and African-American Studies, and the dean's office and administrative staff.

Society of the Haunted had access to all hallways and conference rooms, the administrative office on the third floor, and the basement. Beginning with the basement and working their way up, they swept each level before deciding to concentrate their efforts on the third floor, which had held the operating rooms during the building's infirmary days.

During the sweep, the team's psychic, Vanessa Hogle, who enters a location not knowing a thing about its history and rumored hauntings, felt, "like I was in a crowded auditorium with multiple people yelling, 'Pick me! Pick me!' It all made sense when I was told after the fact that the place we were investigating was once an infirmary."

When it was revealed to Vanessa that the building had once served in this medical capacity, one of the audio recorders the team carried picked up an electronic voice phenomenon of a woman's voice stating, "Sorry." Electronic voice phenomena are believed to be the voices of spirits captured with electronic audio recording equipment.

Activity on the third floor picked up as the night went on. Case manager Cathy Nance reported, "Standing by room 305 I kept hearing knocking on the wall. We could not figure out where the knocking was coming from but it was between another investigator and I. The photographer also verified that he heard the noises as well. I also heard shuffling and something ran past me and bumped into the door. I felt cold air rush past me as I heard noises along the wall. I stayed as [parapsychologist Logan Corelli] went to see where it went. After he went through the door the knocking continued in the same location. I also heard shuffling of papers and chairs moving, and a light which had been off earlier came on at the other end of the hall on the third floor."

Another light that mysterious turned on was in one of the second floor restrooms, possibly confirming one of the reported occurrences. While this was being investigated, the sounds of someone walking around the first floor and doors opening and closing filtered up to the open second floor lounge, but upon inspection by some of the university's yearbook staff on hand to document the investigation and Andrew Shanor, Society of the Haunted's videographer, not a soul was found.

Was the ghost of the roller skating boy found that night? Thus far, the evidence gathered does not prove nor disprove the presence of the legendary skater. Spirits don't act on cue, but an alternative suggestion about the skating sounds was offered by Vanessa: they could be the sounds of hospital bed wheels. Further investigation of the building may reveal more truth.

Watching Over

Judy McCollough

Let me start off by saying my paranormal experiences would not be considered hair raising or jaw dropping or something that would keep you up at night. Mine are a human experience.

At the time I was experiencing some of these we were living in Bay City, Texas, a small town very close to the gulf coast. After my husband's death, I moved back to north Texas for educational reasons, and some of my grown children remained in Bay City.

In 1997, my husband passed away after a battle with cancer. He told me he was not ready to leave this world and fought hard to stay here, but the cancer finally ravaged his body and he lost the fight. He made several references to me that if he died, he would not be far and would be watching over us.

While my husband was ill, I had to continue to work. I wanted to make sure that if he needed me for any reason that would have been an emergency, he would have a way to contact me right away. This was a time before cell phones became so popular and pagers were something many people carried to let someone know they were trying to reach them. I purchased several pagers, and my husband and I had a special code we came up with for him that he would use if he really needed to contact me while I was at work or on an errand. This way I would know to come home immediately. It was a code that only he and I used.

My first paranormal encounter that I believed at the time was coming by way of my husband was about two days after his passing. I was in my bedroom and I had laid some money out on my bed, earmarking it for different expenses that I had to pay for concerning his funeral and other expenses. As I was determining what would go where, all of a sudden, his pager that was lying next to the bed went off.

I went over to look at who was paging him, thinking whoever it was had not realized he had died, and I saw our special code that only he and I used showing on it. It startled me, and I tossed the pager on to the bed, stunned. I did not know what to think. I sat back down on the bed and was finishing up what I was doing, when something came to mind that made me question if my husband was actually there with me in spirit.

While he was living, every time I paid bills or was dealing with money, he had me take care of it all, but he always wanted to see where the money was going just so he knew what was going on, financially. So, even though I really had not dealt with what I thought to be a spirit or ghost, I wondered if my husband was there letting me know he was watching me with the money, and he wanted to see what was going where. I wanted to believe he was still there with me, but soon I just kind of let go of the thought and figured the pager incident was a fluke.

Later that night as I got ready for bed and laid down and was thinking about how much I missed him being there next to me, out of the corner of my eye I saw what appeared to be someone walk past the bed and then quickly disappeared as I turned to get a better look. For a few seconds, I thought I had seen my husband, but then I thought my mind was probably playing tricks on me because I had been thinking of him. I noticed that the room cooled down suddenly, so I covered up with a blanket, turned off the TV, and went to sleep.

The following day family started arriving to attend his upcoming funeral. His niece had come to the house and was visiting. I told her I needed to go to the funeral home to take care of some last-minute preparations and asked if she wanted to come along. She said, "No," and would stay behind and do dishes that had been used for breakfast. We left and went to the funeral home.

When we returned, his niece was sitting on the back bumper of her car in the driveway. I asked why she was sitting outside on her bumper when it was so hot outside (being August heat) and not inside where it was cool. She said she did not want to go back in the house. I asked her why, and she told me that when she was in the kitchen doing dishes she suddenly heard laughing like someone was sitting there at the kitchen table. She said she believed it was my husband because he had a distinct laugh we all loved, and that is what she'd heard. It scared her, so she rushed out of the house and would not go back inside. She said she did not like ghosts. We chatted for a bit and then she left to go visit her grandmother.

We did not know what to think and just laughed about it, but it really started making me second guess everything I had been experiencing.

Later that evening when talking to one of the sons that was staying with us at the time, I explained what his niece said she thought she heard in the kitchen, the son stated that he was thinking about his dad the night before when he was lying on his bed, and he said he felt like someone was touching him like they were trying to console him. After discussing it, we agreed that there were just some things that could not be explained.

The next day was the funeral, and after that everything seemed to go back to normal and no more experiences.

Fast foward two years later.

I was still living in north Texas and decided to make a trip to the gulf coast to visit my kids who were still living there. Before making the trip of over 400 miles, I had asked that my guardian angels watch over me so that I would have a safe trip with no problems since I would be driving and would be alone. I specifically asked that my husband watch over me if that was possible. I packed up the car and set off on my journey.

I had driven all day and I was about 30 minutes away from my destination when a thought came to me that I should stop and get some Benadryl for allergies since I had not been in this area for a while, and to pick up a few goodies for my grandsons whom I would soon be seeing. I stopped at a Walgreens in Wharton, Texas.

The parking spaces at the front of the store were full, so I parked around the side of the building, got out, and went in and made my purchase.

I grabbed my bag of goodies and headed to my car. I opened the car door, and I was making room to place the bag on the seat of the front passenger side. I was leaning over the seats and I heard a horn honk. I thought to myself, quickly, that someone was wanting into the parking spot next to me and I had the door opened too much. I raised up and pulled my head out of the car to let them know I was going to get in the car. I noticed when I looked, no one was next to me but there was a car behind my car that was sitting there parked sideways right behind my car. I could see inside the car clearly from the passenger side, and when I saw the driver, I froze. I could not move or speak for a few seconds.

In that car was my late husband behind the wheel. He was looking right at me and he smiled. I smiled back and my heart felt like it was going to burst. I could not believe who I was looking at. Quickly, I turned my head to see if there was anyone else around seeing this. It only took a second and I turned back to walk over to the car he was in, but it had just vanished. I gasped and cried out for him to come back. I kept waiting and nothing.

I got in my car and just kept saying, "Come back, come back," as if I could will him back if I tried hard enough. After ten minutes, I finally gave up. I had started to cry at some point, so I dried my eyes and decided I needed to go ahead and get to my destination before it got dark. I was shaken, but knew I needed to calm myself so I could drive safely.

As I started to drive off, something dawned on me. I had asked earlier that morning before starting on my trip that my husband watch over me if it was possible. I realized then that he had been watching over me, and he appeared to me to let me know he had been there following me in his ghost car just as I had asked for him to be, and that I was going to be ok for the rest of the trip. It all made sense to me then, and a calm came over me for the rest of the trip.

Once I got to my kids' house, they asked me how my trip went. At first, I was a little hesitant to say anything about what had happened, but decided to tell them. They said they were not surprised. In fact, they had incidences where they believed he was there with them sometimes as well.

My late husband loved gardening and also had a passion for cooking. The kids told me one time they all left the house to run some errands, and when they came home and went inside the house, it was filled with the aroma of food cooking with smells they recognized from when my husband would cook. The first time it happened, they went all around the house looking to find who was there that had been cooking. But no one was there and there was no food anywhere that had been cooked. They went outside and looked around and found nothing, and they only smelled it inside their home. That happened several times.

They would also smell cigar smoke sometimes, and my husband did smoke cigars from time to time. They also said they would hear things in the house sometimes, but could not find anything to explain it. So, when I told them about my experience about the car they did not doubt it for a minute.

It has been almost 20 years since his passing. There were other things at times that I related to it being my husband letting me know he was watching over me. I have not had anything happen in the last five years that would make me feel he is still close. He may still be watching over us, but just not close like he once had been. Has he moved on to the next journey we take after leaving this earthly plane?

In 2005, after experiencing some of these things brought about by my late husband, and some quite unusual experiences that were happening at a workplace at which I was employed, I started doing a little research and became a paranormal researcher/ investigator for eight years. I cannot say I was ever a non-believer, but I had just not had any paranormal experiences until after my husband had passed. I can now say from everything that I have experienced and seen and felt that without a doubt I do believe in the paranormal and that there does seem to be a life after death.

A Raggedy Tale

Wendee Whittington

I remember it like it was yesterday... 40 years later. A popular doll back in the 70s was the Raggedy Ann doll. She came in all sizes and I had the child life sized version. I adored her and she slept beside me every night. Now, I say I adored her and I really did... but discovering life as a clairvoyant child I began to notice something a little off about my beloved doll. It wasn't long before adoration turned to fear.

To add a bit of a backstory, the home in which I was raised during these years was extremely active with an energy that, to this day, I shudder to think back to. My clairvoyant abilities were just starting to open to me, and whatever was in our home knew full well that I knew it was there. It also knew what scared me, and it used it. The doll was number one in its arsenal.

The encounter happened one night when I was seven years old. I had taken to pushing the doll out of the bed during the night, watching with pleasure as she hit the floor. This night was like all the other nights I did this. Smiling with satisfaction as the cloth body met the wood slabs below, I turned over and started to drift off.

Bump... shake... rustle…

My eyes flew open. Wide. I remember how bright the moon seemed to be. My heart was racing, my breath barely daring to escape as I was listening for any further noises, feeling for more sensations. One major factor here... I was born quadriplegic and could not run. Or leave the bed – period.

"What was that?" My mind started racing with what to do. Should I look? Should I scream? Would there be time for anyone to come? This house was dangerous and it knew I was helpless to escape.

I decided to look behind me.

There she lied, eyes meeting mine in a coal black dead on stare! Her painted on smile met my wide-eyed, open mouthed, terrified face. Not only was she right back in her place next to me, she was unnaturally positioned on her side, as if to let me know what she'd done.

I did scream. I kept screaming. I pushed her again. I watched the doll fall for a second time that night. And when my mother finally opened the door all I could do was cry and tell her to take Raggedy Ann away.

Years later, I learned of the doll's rather dark history and why she was made, and most of all… another haunting in which a Raggedy Ann doll was used and manipulated as mine had been. Her name was Annabelle.

From that night on my Raggedy Ann doll stayed in the guest room closet.

On the floor. In the corner. In the dark. Where she belonged.

Wendee is a 47 year old artist, web designer, singer, and an avid paranormal seeker. She grew up in Ohio. Both homes in her childhood were high in paranormal activity but the one in which her encounter above took place was by far the worst, a little house on Ravenwood Ave. To this day she has no idea why the home was the way it was. She has no information of its history, only memories... and that's enough.

Parental Visitations

Cheryal Hussain

Just after my mother passed in March 1992, my son was home alone. He said that the spirit of his grandmother had appeared to him, accompanied with my father. He had died in 1981, before my son was born. They appeared to be young, although they died older. He described their clothing down to my father's gold rimmed glasses he wore laid out in his casket and the brocaded wedding dress my mother wore. My mother was in her 70s when she died, but my son described her as very young.

When he came and told me, there was no one else in the house, but the scent of Lilly Of The Valley perfume, which was my mother's favorite perfume that she wore for as long as I could remember, was floating in the air. I would like to think that she was introducing my son to his grandfather. My son was born long after my father's death. It can be said that it was a loving visitation.

In the early morning hours of the death of my father; I had a dream. In that dream a very strong voice said, "Your father is dead."

There was a pitch-dark void and that message. The voice was so strong that I was shocked awake. Later that morning, it was confirmed that my father had died in the early morning hours. Was it a premonition?

On the night of my mother's funeral one of my sister-in-laws who was close to my mother had dream that she was in a dark house with many rooms. In one of those rooms she saw a body lying on the floor in the fetal position. The body was illuminated in light. As my sister-in-law drew close enough to touch the body, the head turned and she was looking into the face of my mother. My mother looked at my sister-in-law and told her she did not like being dead. My sister-in-law was scared and started running in her dream. My Mother was running behind her, and just as she caught up to my sister-in-law, my sister-in-law woke up.

The next day we cooked a sweet dish and prayed over it for the soul of my mother. The next night I had a dream, as well, about my mother. I dreamt that I was walking up to my mother's home, I knocked on the door, and she answered all dressed up to go out. The house was all lit up and comfortable looking as it was when she was alive. I came in and just as I stepped in, my mother said, "Wait outside. I'm going to check the gas." She always did that before she went out. So, I went outside to wait for her, and that is when I woke up.

I would like to think that she was trying to tell us everything was going to be ok. It was after a few years that the incident with my son happened.

Top 11
Paranormal Frauds

Mike Ricksecker

This "chapter" is more like the anti-encouter, an account of those that have claimed to have had a paranormal experience or to have done something supernatural only to have been proven a hoax to one degree or another. Unfortunately, they do exist, but just because some people fake a paranormal or supernatural experience, it doesn't mean that all accounts are false. These are cases of those few spoiling it for the many whom have had real encounters and are a part of the reason why many are so skeptical of those that come forward with what they've seen.

Article originally published as a blog post December 7, 2015 at http://www.mikericksecker.com/blog

While I have witnessed some truly remarkable paranormal activity, there have been a number of people throughout the years that have created their own paranormal or supernatural hoax in order to fool the masses. While this list I've compiled isn't nowhere near complete, it is at least a compelling selection spanning hundreds (sometimes thousands) of years to consider worthy of the Top 11 historic paranormal frauds. Below is the video to accompany this blog article:

11. The Cottingly Fairies

The Cottingly Fairies were a series of photographs taken in 1917 and 1920 by cousins Frances Griffith and Elsie Wright depicting them playing with fairies. The 1920 photos were actually commissioned by an unaware Sir Arthur Conan Doyle of Sherlock Holmes fame. While blatantly fraudulent to our modern eye, photographic experts of the day declared the photos genuine and the hoax continued on for decades. It wasn't until 1981 that Elsie finally admitted that the fairies were paper cutouts of sketches she had drawn inspired by Princess Mary's Gift Book.

10. Rudolph Fentz

Rudolph Fentz was a time traveler, appearing out of the blue in 1950 dressed in 19th Century garb in New York City's Time Square, freaked out, and ran into traffic where he was accidentally killed by a car. Money in his pocket was from the 1800s and business cards identifying him were confirmed by the widow of

Ralph Fentz Jr. who stated that her father-in-law vanished without a trace in 1876. This tale was popular for decades, especially in Europe's paranormal circles, but that makes sense considering the truth. This tale was actually a story in a 1951 science fiction anthology, but was reprinted two years later as a "true story" in a booklet describing "proof" of a fourth dimension, which found its way to Europe where it took a strong hold.

9. Peter Popoff

Peter Popoff was a faith healer during the 1980s who had a penchant for announcing the home addresses and specific illnesses of audience members, and was raking in millions while doing it. He was revealed as a fraud when it was discovered he was using a wireless ear receiver to be fed the information.

8. Mumler's Spirit Photography

During the 1860s, William Mumler rose to fame as a spirit photographer, the first of which was a self-portrait which also contained the image of a young girl who looked eerily similar to his cousin who had passed away. As the photo made the rounds his popularity grew, and throughout his career he imaged some 500 spirit photos for clients, including one of Mary Todd Lincoln depicting her husband, President Abraham Lincoln, behind her. Mumler was taken to court for fraud and ruining the reputation of photographers, the prosecution showing that the effect could easily be achieved using double negatives. But he was acquitted based on the defense that his clients truly believed the images in the photos were of their deceased loved ones. Nevertheless, his work to this day is considered fraudulent.

7. Alien Autopsy

Billed by Fox television in 1995 as real autopsy footage shot just after the infamous Roswell UFO crash, Alien Autopsy was aired insinuating that everything that was shown was, in fact, real. And while the look and feel of the footage appeared real, it was far from it. Under the guise of "recreations", the footage was actually shot in a London flat with two alien dummy bodies containing sheep brains in raspberry jam, chicken entrails, and knuckle joints.

6. The Ghostly Drummer of Tedworth

The Tedworth Drummer has made two appearances in history. The first was in 1661 at the home of John Monpesson in Wiltshire, England who claimed an angry drumming spirit had invaded his home after he'd had a drummer's drum confiscated for collecting money under false pretenses. The case became famous throughout England and the drummer was also charged with the crime of employing an evil spirit, but many have pointed that no one was ever allowed to inspect the cellar of Monpesson's home, the drumming almost always happened at night, and an investigation sanctioned by the King revealed nothing. The second appearance was in Philadelphia in 1730 through a letter to the Pennsylvania Gazette which claimed two local Reverends had recently encountered an angry, drum-beating ghost being "not a whit less obstreperous than the Tedworth Tympanist." Most believe the letter, and a second follow up defending the Reverends, were part of an extended hoax by Benjamin Franklin, who was the publisher.

5. The Amityville Horror

The real horror at Amityville was the murder of six members of the DeFeo family in 1974. A best-selling book and a series of movies sensationalized the paranormal horror story told by the Lutz's who moved in afterward, which continues to be discounted, but remains popular even after lawyer William Weber admitted to knowing the book was a hoax and he helped create the horror story with the Lutz's over many bottles of wine.

4. Uri Geller

Uri Geller became famous in the 1970s for his mind-reading tricks and mind-powered spoon bending, swearing that he had true psychic powers to make these things happen and became a huge sensation. He was then outed in front of millions on The Johnny Carson Show when Johnny (who just happened to be a former magician) made sure Geller did not bring his own props and presented him a table full of spoons and other objects for him to manipulate. Geller stalled and went silent, ultimately fleeing the situation by claiming he didn't feel strong that night.

3. Salem Witches

The Salem Witch trials are the most tragic on this list since it involved the execution of 20 people, mostly women, in and around Salem, Massachusetts in the 1690s. It started when a group of young girls claimed to be possessed by the devil and accused several local women of witchcraft then put on a display of spams, screams, and contortions in court. Mass hysteria spread throughout the area and up to 150 women, men, and children were actually accused over several months. One theory proposes that the delusions, vomiting, and muscle spasms may have been an effect of the fungus ergot.

2. The Fox Sisters

The Fox sisters were sensationalized through newspapers accounts in the mid-1800s and, later, PT Barnum who made them national

celebrities as the modern Spiritualism movement when they displayed that they could communicate with spirits through rapping sounds on a table. They cultivated a large following which still exists to this day, while the Society for Psychical Research worked to expose them as frauds. Finally, in 1888, Margaret Fox confessed to the fraud in a signed letter that she and her two sisters sought to terrify their mother when they were children and developed the method for making the noises, which is what they employed during their séances.

1. Simon Magus (Simon the Sorcerer, Simon the Magician)

During the very beginning of Christianity, Simon was traveling the countryside and claiming to be the great power of God through his magic arts. He was baptized into Christianity, but as he continued to witness the miracles performed by the apostles he offered them money and demanded he be shown how to produce their magic so he could enhance his "powers", his show. He was rebuked by Peter and became a nemesis to the apostles. The apocrypha contains accounts of Simon Magus rising in power and seeking to win the favor of Emperor Nero, which was ultimately thwarted. Writers of the early church universally represent him as the first heretic and the "Father of Heresies." A fraud.

THE GOLDENROD SHOWBOAT

A Vignette of American History

W. R. MARKLE'S NEW SHOW BOAT

THE LARGEST, FINEST AND MOST COMPLETE SHOW BOAT IN THE WORLD

The Goldenrod Showboat was the biggest and most luxurious showboat ever to entertain along the Mississippi River during the golden age of America's rag time era. Built in 1909, traveled the Mid West's rivers, from Pittsburg to Omaha, until 1937 where Captain Bill Menke found a permanent home along the St. Louis waterfront for nearly 53 years, offering a plethora of melodramas and entertainment. The Goldenrod was declared a National Historic Landmark in 1967, and it sat in front of the Gateway Arch from the time of its construction until 1983. In 1989, the city of St. Charles purchased the showboat, and it entertained there along the Missouri River until 2001 when the Goldenrod ran aground due to changing water levels and repairs were deemed too costly. The iconic showboat ended up on the shores of the Illinois River in Kampsville where it remained in limbo until a 2017 arson fire destroyed it.

Goldenrod Goodbye
More Than Just Ghosts

This article, posted March 28, 2016, was a memorial to the historic showboat which was on the verge of shutting its doors forever on April 1. It has since been saved…and lost again (please see Foreword and www.goldenrodshowboat.com for details).

It's so much more than ghosts. To gaze upon a relic is to infuse yourself with everything that relic has come to represent: the people, the era, the ambience. History in today's society has been relegated to the monotonous memorization of names and dates of people to which we believe we have no connection. We have forgotten the world as it once was, lost in the grind of our breakneck society while traversing what had once been countryside through concrete monstrosities and lifeless asphalt. And so, when one of those relics is greeted with the demise of a scrap pile death, such as the historic Goldenrod Showboat, most don't even bat a manicured eye at its imminent destruction.

It was a jewel on the Mississippi River, the largest and most luxurious showboat ever constructed. Red Skelton got his start there and other famous talents performed on its stage, such as Bob Hope. Do those names even resonate with people anymore? For nearly 100 years the Goldenrod provided laughter and life for thousands along the old waterway, providing a means of escapism from life along the river, but now it rests on shore, a rusting hulk replete of its previous grandeur. Must we allow ourselves to forget all that has come before us?

Stand still for a moment and listen to the lap of the water against the shore and the breeze gently caress the leaves of nearby trees. Open your eyes and stare not at your cell phone but at the gentle ripple of a wave or the delicate veins of a leaf. For just a moment lead not with your persuasive techniques or heavy hand in the corporate boardroom, but lead with your senses. Where does it take you? Does anyone look at the stars anymore or have they become so blotted out by the false light of our street lamps that no one even bother to look?

From the deck of the Goldenrod, resting in Kampsville, Illinois, I finally understood why the ancients so revered the celestial heavens. That night, the darkest sky I have ever experienced produced the brightest stars in the highest abundance I have ever seen. For the first time I saw the constellation Orion in its full glory flanked by so many other brilliant twinkling skylights that I almost couldn't discern it. One word describes the moment and even it doesn't do that moment justice: amazing. The night sky greeted me with a sensuous kiss that I have longed to return.

Make no mistake that I enjoy having my car to travel from place to place and my computer is currently making this article possible, but having modern conveniences doesn't mean we should forget the past and the world around us. Locations like the Goldenrod Showboat are a time capsule, a vessel to take us to a place we've left behind. The encompassing energy when one steps inside its main doors instantly whisks you away to that forgotten era of ragtime and authentic melodrama, making you drunk on escapism within escapism if you allow it. It's a pure looking glass into that time of American history without the overzealous pandering of modern commercialism.

Soon the Goldenrod will be gone. Whatever doesn't get salvaged for scrap will be burned, adding further insult to injury as longtime owner, Captain Bill Menke, pieced a significant portion of the boat back together by hand after a fire in St. Louis in 1962 when he was more than 80 years old. To this day his spirit still roams his life's passion, literally going down with the ship.

In the end the Goldenrod Showboat will be a footnote in history, relegated to a few paragraphs on a dusty webpage with a few museum items kept on-hand by those who truly cared for it. Hopefully, it will be remembered for a bit more than just a few names and dates — for the best history teachers are storytellers. And its ghost stories that they tell.

Mike Ricksecker is the author of the historic paranormal books *Ghosts of Maryland* and *Ghosts and Legends of Oklahoma* and the hybrid paranormal research series *Ghostorian Case Files*. He has appeared on Animal Planet's *The Haunted* and Bio Channel's *My Ghost Story*, Fox 5 News (Washington DC) and Coast-to-Coast AM, and he produces his own Internet shows "Ghosts and Legends" and "Paranormal Roads" on Haunted Road Media's YouTube channel. Additionally, Mike is an Amazon best-selling mystery author with two entries to his Chase Michael DeBarlo private detective series, *Deadly Heirs* and *System of the Dead*. Visit his web site at: www.mikericksecker.com

Life Entwined With A Showboat

Shana Wankel

If anyone had told me years ago that my life would someday become entwined with an abandoned showboat and the spirits that inhabited it, I would've questioned their sanity. That's exactly what happened, however, and my life is richer because of it.

The Goldenrod Showboat was built in 1909 and was the biggest and most elaborately decorated vessel of its kind. It boasted melodramas, vaudeville acts, music, and dancing. Basking in the glow of those stage lights is where performers such as Red Skelton and Bob Hope got their start. It was also the home of Captain Bill Menke, who loved that boat with his whole heart and shed more than his fair share of blood, sweat, and tears aboard it. Captain Menke died in the place he loved most.

The boat was also home to "Annie," who has also gone by the names "Victoria" and "Rose" over the years. Annie met with an untimely death floating next to the vessel, and although the details aren't certain, it appeared that foul play may have played a part in her demise.

The boat's fate was to travel upriver to a sleepy, river town called Kampsville, Illinois, where it remains to this day. Events took place that led me and a group of other dedicated people to become caretakers of the showboat. From my very first time stepping aboard the boat, I knew that my time spent in the days to come would be the stuff that my dreams were made of. As a paranormal investigator, it's a veritable gold mine of activity.

I remember the afternoon very well. I was onboard with other caretakers to give a tour to a group that had taken an interest in the boat, its history, and paranormal activity. The group had wandered into the theater while I decided to sneak off upstairs into what was recently a dining area, but was formerly the living quarters for the staff. In no way, shape, or form, did I anticipate what would take place next.

I had brought my audio recorder with me, because I never went anywhere without it. I turned it on and sat it down.

Interacting with Annie and Captain Menke always seemed to happen naturally and felt good. I always asked them how they were doing, if they minded that we brought new people to meet them, and other random questions just to make small talk. I've always been able to rely on my "spidey sense," as I referred to it, to let me know before something was going to happen, whether it was bad or just significant.

Annie overwhelmed me from out of nowhere and with no warning. It was like a full body takeover, emotionally, and to this day, I'm not sure if I was feeling her emotions as "her," *or* if I was just saddened because she, herself, was sad. Regardless, it felt like my world had come crashing down around me. I was overcome by grief and cried like my heart was breaking. I remember taking a deep breath and exhaling to try to regain some composure and control of the situation.

Once I had my wits about me again, even though I was still crying, I ran over and grabbed my recorder. I immediately started asking her questions. I asked her why she was so sad today and what it was that she was trying to tell me. I instinctively *knew* that it was her and *not* Captain Menke. I've *always* been able to discern between the two of them. Eventually, I couldn't handle the emotional energy and ran downstairs, throwing out an apology for my departure and saying that I'd return.

I flew down the stairs and ran into the theater where the rest of the group was. I'm *sure* I made quite an impression and likely spooked a few of them. One of the other caretakers, my friend, Becca, was there to offer up some comfort and some Reiki. Reiki, of course, is healing through touch and positive energy, and after my encounter with Annie on that day, it was exactly what the doctor ordered.

To this day, I've not had quite the same encounter with Annie as I had that day. Yes, she still alerts me of her presence, but not quite so strongly.

Captain Menke and I, however, have a different kind of bond. We are kindred spirits, he and I, and have had quite an interesting friendship aboard that vessel. I feel him all over that boat and especially in his private quarters. I feel quite privileged that he's allowed me to see him, that he's called me out by name, and has even professed to missing me when I'm not around, by offering up a "miss you" on my recorder. I treasure that EVP always.

I could talk for days about my experiences aboard the grand dame and I highly recommend that everyone visit her, if they get the chance.

Annie

Mike Ricksecker

I believe I first encountered Annie in the main lobby and concession area of the Goldenrod Showboat. I had ventured inside with my video camera in hand and was left alone for a few minutes to soak up the atmosphere. I love moments like these and being given a chance to just listen to and feel a particular location. I could certainly feel the age of the boat around me, its golden years gone by, but I could also feel that it still had some life in her yet. That's when I felt her near me.

I was looking out toward the windows, wondering what the splendor of the showboat must've looked like back in its glory days, when I felt a presence approach me. At first I thought it might have been Shana, but I knew she was back out on the deck with Jake. I turn from side to side, but nobody was there, and I suddenly felt a slight tickle behind my ear, a distinct sensation as if somebody was lightly playing with my hair. Whoever it was, it felt female in nature, and as quickly as the sensation had come it had gone.

Of course, this could have been anybody, but after what happened later that evening I do believe that this brief encounter was Annie saying, "Hello."

Annie has been young woman who lived on the Goldenrod Showboat many years beforehand in St. Louis along with her father who worked there. While she dreamt of being on stage, she had a fling with the assistant captain who encouraged her to perform as an actress and a dancer like many of the others who worked there.

One night, her involvement with the assistant captain came to a head as her father expressly forbade her from seeing the man. An argument ensued between father and daughter, and Annie ran off the boat into the dark St. Louis night. The next morning, she was found as a corpse floating alongside the Goldenrod, and to this day nobody knows what truly happened to her that fateful evening.

Later that evening I'd visited, Shana and I were deep into our paranormal investigation of the Goldenrod, and we were exploring the second floor dining and dance area which is purported to be a frequent haunt of the spirit known as Annie. Since Annie is known to enjoy dancing, I asked her if she would like to dance with me on the small patch of wooden floor in the center of the room. I'm not a very good dancer, so I did my best to amble about in a circular fashion as Shana looked on. That's when I felt it.

Similar to what I had experienced on the lower deck, I felt the sensation of somebody playing with my right ear and the hair around it. I laughed a little since it did tickle a little bit, and I told Shana about what I was experiencing.

Playfully, Shana spotted an opportunity for the spirit to get a little more interactive and suggested, "Annie, if you like his ear so much why don't you go ahead and blow in it?"

Sure enough, at that prompting I felt a sudden burst of air inside my right ear as if somebody had just puckered their lips and blown directly into it. I gasped and laughed, "She just did!"

We had a good chuckle, and Shana suggested that Annie do it again. Sure enough, in my other ear I felt the same kind of sudden influx of air as if somebody had just blown into it.

We don't know why this spirit was so forward and interactive that particular night. Perhaps I resembled the young man she had fallen for and was denied pursuing the night her life came to an end. Or, perhaps, she was simply in a happy, playful mood that evening. These are possibilities upon which we would normally follow up; however, we may not have that opportunity with Annie.

Just before the Goldenrod closed its doors at the end of March 2016, a medium was brought on board in order to afford the opportunity for spirits to pass on before the boat was to be destroyed. Annie was, purportedly, one of the spirits that did so. In a follow-up investigation of the Goldenrod after it re-opened its doors, I made another attempt to dance with Annie in the same location in which she had blown into my ear. Something did happen, and it wasn't Annie... but that is another story for another time.

Final Ceremony
Handfasting on the Goldenrod
10/29/2016

The Scream

Shana Wankel

As an Empath, spending time on the Goldenrod Showboat has always been one of the best ways to explore my abilities. Some Empaths are able to sense the emotions of those still amongst the living, but I've always been more in tune with the emotions, thoughts, and actions of those who have already passed on into the next realm. Sometimes I tune in when I'm physically at the place where the energy is, and sometimes it comes to me in my mind or in dreams when I'm at home.

It was a regular night at home and I had fallen asleep. At around 1am, I was woken up by the sound of someone screaming for me to help them. My gut instinct had me running to check on my kids first, but they were sound asleep. As I stopped to gather myself and tune in a little better, I started to get the familiar feeling of having been visited by someone in the metaphysical way. Who was it? As hard as I tried, I just could not get a lockdown on who it was or where it was coming from. After some time, I fell back asleep, but it wasn't easy and I felt like something was off.

When I woke up the next morning, I saw news that turned my world upside down. My beloved Goldenrod Showboat had been set ablaze and was destroyed. I went through a series of emotions including shock, grief, and anger. Then, I remembered what had awoken me in the middle of the night. The scream for help, I believe, belonged to one of the spirits of the Goldenrod. Or, was it the boat itself?

Today, this senseless act has bolstered our efforts to help saved endangered, historic places from destruction. It's a labor of love and quite frustrating at times. Those of us who care do all that we can with the resources that we have, but sometimes it's just not enough, and these amazing places are lost to us with just memories remaining. I have not visited the site of the final resting place of the Goldenrod Showboat yet, but you can bet that it's on my to-do list. By the time some of you read this book, it may have already happened, so watch for updates about it on our social media pages.

Not only was the showboat a home for spirits like Captain Bill Menke, Charlie Menke, and Annie, but there were also other energies as well. Were they attached to the boat itself or to the land that it sat on? Remember our tales of yellow balls of light and twinkling anomalies (*Encounters With The Paranormal: Volume 3*)? Who and what are they, what is their role as it relates to the showboat and the land itself, and will we ever find the answers we seek?

I'm not sure what the future holds for the memory of the Goldenrod, but it will forever remain a part of my heart and soul, and if you ever want to hear the stories of its life and impact on my life, you know where to find me.

Charley

Mike Ricksecker

It was supposed to be our next great investigative project on the Goldenrod Showboat before it all went up in an inferno. We had always felt a presence in the back corridor on the second floor, and we were determined to learn more about it even while we had started investigating the possibility of fairy activity on the Goldenrod following our November 2016 "Ghosts of the Goldenrod" event (*see Encounters With The Paranormal: Volume 3*). In a vessel out in the middle of nowhere, on a boat completely devoid of power, it's difficult to find a "real world" explanation for the feel of static electricity or that encroaching heaviness always felt within that area.

I felt it there in my first jaunt through, part of a tour of the historic showboat when I visited in February, 2016. The moment we slid past the door leading from the balcony, the lingering heaviness pressed upon me. It was male. Commanding. Yet, it was also dark and sad.

By no means, do I claim to be a psychic medium, but I can feel where there is an unseen presence in the room, and sometimes I can gauge the type of demeanor it's presenting.

To say that corridor had some energy is an understatement. We toss the term around sometimes as paranormal investigators, an easy way to describe the sensation of something almost electrical enveloping you, but in the case of the second floor back corridor of the Goldenrod Showboat, it was much more than just a feeling. A presence engulfed the entire small room.

I said nothing of it to Shana. We had just met, and I was there as a visiting investigator, writer, and videographer. But I wouldn't always stay silent about the matter.

Time and time again since then, we have passed through that short corridor, and nearly every time the presence was there. Sometimes, we would also hear footsteps, on occasion a voice or a whisper, and one time a small mist of light that fluttered into view for the video camera (see "Haunted Goldenrod Showboat Final Investigations: Part 1 at youtube.com/hauntedroadmedia).

Other times, we saw a shadow figure pass through the doorway. On one particular occasion, when Shana witnessed a shadow pass through the doorway she also observed two "twinkles" follow it inside.

Unfortunately, we never did discover what exactly the twinkles were, but toward the final days we were seeing more of them throughout the showboat – tiny pinpricks of light that would flash and then, just as quickly, extinguish. We have to hope we can find those twinkles elsewhere to learn their secret.

A secret of a different kind was ultimately revealed to us was on our very last investigation of the Goldenrod before she was lost. After all that time, we were finally informed that in the original configuration of the second floor, that short passageway in which we kept experiencing that activity had originally been the quarters of Charley Menke.

Charley Menke was the brother of Captain Bill Menke, and was a longtime assistant captain himself. In fact, he had been the assistant captain with which young Victoria Anne – Annie – had had her fateful fling.

The original configuration of the Goldenrod featured a central corridor that ran from the balcony through what became the dining area, but back in the day it had been the staff quarters (except for Captain Bill who had his own apartment on the second floor behind the stage). From the balcony, the first room on the right belonged to Charley. But in the final renovation, the central passageway was removed to make way for the galley, and the entranceway was move to a single door on the right side of the balcony. Passing through it led straight through the heart of what had been Charley's quarters.

So, if the energy there – the shadow and the presence – had been Charley, what did he want? Why did he linger there? Was he heartbroken about the condition of the boat he and his brothers had operated for so long? Was he heartbroken about Annie? Perhaps he was even guilt-ridden that her involvement with him ultimately led to her demise.

These are questions with which we would have followed up had we been able continue our investigations. That opportunity is now gone, lost in a short-sighted blaze of greed. We'll never have the opportunity to walk into Charley Menke's quarters again.

There is one question that remains, however, and it is a sad one to consider. Where is Charley now? Is he still wandering the grounds where the Goldenrod was set afire? Has he returned to the St. Louis area where he spent most of his says aboard the showboat, and where Annie was lost? Has he found solace in the home of descendants? Or has he ventured to the "world beyond," wherever that may be?

Unfortunately, we may never know.

The Twins' Farewell

Shana Wankel

What more can be said about the Goldenrod Showboat that I haven't already said? I've had many wonderful experiences aboard that grand dame. As a paranormal investigator, if someone told me that I had to pick just one venue to investigate for the rest of my days, it would have been the showboat. Unfortunately, I now find myself saying "would have been" rather than "would be", since the tragic destruction of the vessel has taken it away. It now remains as a pile of ruins and memories. The story I'm telling today will be about two wonderful ladies who I've known for many years, our experiences aboard the boat, and the amazing memento that they gifted me with for Christmas this year.

One of my favorite things to do aboard the boat was be with people who shared my love for the history and the spirits that lived there. My two guests, Tammy and Tonya Hayn, are childhood friends and twins who went to school with me many moons ago. These ladies are genuinely good souls with bright energy, infectious smiles, and loads of love and light. The energy that twins have has always fascinated me. Their metaphysical bond with each other and how it meshes with paranormal energy is a subject that I'm eager to explore and research.

It was a treat to watch them react to the different energies that the boat was producing. Even more exciting was that there were several times when all three of us had shared experiences. As we slowly wandered down into the showroom, the same feelings of awe assailed me. When you descend the five steps that lead to the walkway going into the showroom, the energy changes. The roof of the second story balcony is above you and as soon as you clear it, the boat just opens up and this giant room hits you. You can almost feel the lingering energy from the shows and the crowds who came to see them. After a few seconds, my body learns to shield that energy and focus on single energies from the dominant spirits of the showboat.

We spent a lot of our time in the showroom talking about all of the experiences that had been had there, and even indulged in stories of experiences that had happened in other venues and in our private lives at home. Activity kind of started picking up during our storytelling and we started hearing movement around us and upstairs. I entertained the thought that maybe our resident spirits were fans of storytelling and were coming closer to enjoy it with us. As we were standing in the center of the room, the ladies saw a fast-moving, dark shadow figure moving down lower to the floor. I didn't share the experience with them at that time and hadn't really expected to. Such is the way of the paranormal most of the time, because not everyone shares experiences with others, which sometimes makes it hard to prove. However, this time luck was on my side.

As my eyes were scouring the area where they had seen the shadow, all of a sudden, a dark shadow manifested close to me down low in the same place they had witnessed the anomaly. It was about a foot long, half a foot wide, and black in color. It just appeared without warning, moved fast towards a small, wooden post in the floor, and vanished into the post. I jumped and we laughed. I stepped over to the area where the shadow disappeared and it appeared to have been absorbed by the post itself. There was no trace of it to be found and it never appeared again.

We decided to move upstairs and follow up on the sounds we were hearing from downstairs in the showroom. As we were standing upstairs, we discussed what we saw down below and I started telling stories about some of the experiences that have been on the second floor. We all heard a noise coming from behind us in what used to be Charlie Menke's room. Charlie was the assistant captain and the brother of Captain Bill Menke. His room was always one that was hard for me to spend any time in. The feelings were always quite overwhelming due to Charlie's strong energy. Since we didn't see anything, we resumed our conversation that we were having before the noise distracted us. I was standing facing his room and the ladies were standing next to each other in front of me but spaced far enough apart that so that I still had a clear visual of the room. All of a sudden, a bright flash of light appeared in the doorway. It was about the size of a basketball and the color of a flashlight beam. The room it appeared in has no windows, so I was able to at least debunk the theory of it coming from outside sources. Unfortunately, they both turned too late to see it, because it happened so quickly, but we had all heard the noise preceding it.

With the temperatures dropping and free time growing short, we decided to call it a day, with the hopes of returning again soon.

The boat has always been an active spot for me and I loved having shared experiences with these two ladies. Unfortunately, luck isn't always on our side when it comes to being able to get together to explore, and we didn't have another chance to share time on the boat before it was destroyed. They messaged me one day this month on Facebook to tell me that they had a Christmas gift for me. I was so touched by this gesture, because in my eyes, their friendship alone is a gift. We agreed to meet up inside Mineral Springs Hotel and catch up as well.

After we had met and all greeted each other, they handed me a big, glittery, red box with a shiny bow and said that they hoped that it didn't make me sad but that they just wanted to give me something special. I held my breath as I opened the lid and sitting inside was a framed picture of the Goldenrod Showboat that one of their sons had taken from before it's destruction. As if that in itself wasn't special, the picture was sitting on top of a charred piece of the original red wallpaper from the showroom. These ladies had actually risked exploring the rubble of the boat, which was still smoldering in spots at the time, and found this last remnant and gifted it to me.

To say I was touched is putting it mildly. With tears in my eyes, I sat stunned. This gift was their way of saying thanks for me letting them experience the showboat with me. I will treasure this gift and their friendship for the rest of our days on this earth and into the next realms of existence. One thing that my experiences with the boat and with life in general has shown me is that we are not guaranteed tomorrow. Treasure each moment you have with the people and places that you hold dear, because one day, memories may be all that you have.

Conclusion

Mike Ricksecker

It was June 17, 1989, when I first set eyes upon the Goldenrod Showboat, although I didn't know then the significance of what I was looking at. It was there during its 53-year stint in St. Louis, along the water's edge with a few of the other newer showboats. I even spotted it again from the top of the Gateway Arch, although, again, I still didn't realize then that one of the boats below would come to play such a significant part of my life – and not even in St. Louis. This writing predates by a week a handfasting ceremony for Shana and I at the location which brought us together.

Is that somehow paranormal? Supernatural? The Oxford Dictionary defines paranormal as, "Denoting events or phenomena such as telekinesis or clairvoyance that are beyond the scope of normal scientific understanding."

Is it beyond the scope of normal scientific understanding that a showboat once encountered briefly in 1989 played the part in bringing two people together 27 years later at a location an hour away up a different river? Is it beyond the scope of scientific understanding that people who once lived and worked on that showboat can still be heard there, can be felt there, and can even be seen there?

Is it beyond the scope of normal scientific understanding that people have interacted with loved ones that have passed away, have received messages from their former pets, have been terrorized by shadow people in the night, and have received visions over great distances from people that have long since been gone from this plane of existence?

If the answer is, "Yes, those things are beyond the scope of normal scientific understanding," and these encounters and experiences are happening, then why is it so hard for some people to acknowledge that paranormal activity does, indeed, exist?

After all, almost everyone has a ghost story.

Other titles from Haunted Road Media:

Almost everyone has a ghost story. Real people. Real stories.

Read about haunted houses and vehicles, experiences during paranormal investigations, visits from relatives that have passed on, pets reacting to the paranormal, psychic experiences, and conversations with full-bodied apparitions.

ENCOUNTERS WITH THE PARANORMAL reveals personal stories of the supernatural, exploring the realm beyond the veil through the eyes of a colorful cast of contributors.

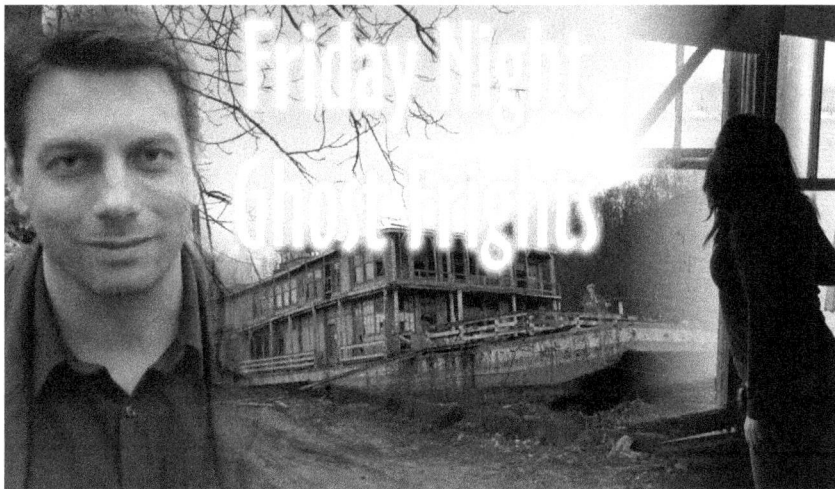

Subscribe at: http://www.youtube.com/hauntedroadmedia

For more information visit:
www.hauntedroadmedia.com

www.ingramcontent.com/pod-product-compliance
Lightning Source LLC
LaVergne TN
LVHW051416080426
835508LV00022B/3108